PENSION SHARING – THE NEW LAW

WELFARE REFORM AND PENSIONS ACT 1999

PENSION SHARING – THE NEW LAW

WELFARE REFORM AND PENSIONS ACT 1999

District Judge Roger Bird LLB

 **Family Law**

1999

Published by
Family Law
a publishing imprint of
Jordan Publishing Limited
21 St Thomas Street
Bristol BS1 6JS

British Library Cataloguing-in-Publication Data

A catalogue record for this book is available
from the British Library.

ISBN 0 85308 589 7

Photoset by Mendip Communications Ltd, Frome, Somerset
Printed in Great Britain by MPG Books, Bodmin, Cornwall

PREFACE

Pension sharing has been a part of the law of this country since an obligation to bring it about was imposed on the then Lord Chancellor in 1996. That this obligation was not accepted with complete enthusiasm is demonstrated by the fact that it is only now that the statutory material has emerged in a final form and it will probably not be until 2001 that the Welfare Reform and Pensions Act 1999 comes into force. The whole process will therefore have taken five years. This clearly has its drawbacks, but one of the advantages may be that practitioners will have had ample time to digest what the future has in store. I hope that this book will make that process relatively painless.

I am very grateful to David Salter for reading the manuscript and suggesting one or two amendments. Needless to say, responsibility for any errors rests with me.

Roger Bird
30 November 1999

CONTENTS

TABLE OF CASES

References are to paragraph numbers.

TABLE OF STATUTES

References are to paragraph numbers or page numbers. References in bold indicate where the text is set out in full.

TABLE OF STATUTORY INSTRUMENTS

References are to paragraph numbers.

TABLE OF ABBREVIATIONS

APP	appropriate personal pension scheme
CETV	cash equivalent transfer value
COMP	contracted-out money purchase scheme
COSR	contracted-out salary-related scheme
FLA 1996	Family Law Act 1996
GMP	guaranteed minimum pension
ICTA 1988	Income and Corporation Taxes Act 1988
MCA 1973	Matrimonial Causes Act 1973
MFPA 1984	Matrimonial and Family Proceedings Act 1984
MFR	minimum funding requirement
NHA	National Health Service
PA 1995	Pensions Act 1995
PSA 1993	Pension Schemes Act 1993
SERPS	State earnings-related pension scheme
WRPA 1999	Welfare Reform and Pensions Act 1999

Chapter 1

THE BACKGROUND TO THE 1999 ACT

INTRODUCTION

1.1   The enactment of the Welfare Reform and Pensions Act 1999 (WRPA 1999) represents both the end of a long campaign by those wishing to bring about this change and the putting into place of an important tool for the courts when making orders for ancillary relief. The importance of pensions as part of the assets which constitute the subject matter of such orders has been recognised for many years. In many cases, after the matrimonial home, the value of one of the parties' pension is the largest single asset, and cannot be ignored when a court dealing with an ancillary relief application decides what is just in the light of the factors contained in s 25(2) of the Matrimonial Causes Act 1973 (MCA 1973). However, this recognition seems to have been gradual; while pension sharing, as it has now come to be enacted, has been a demand of campaigners for some time, the approach of the legislature has lagged behind and it is only now that it can be said that the courts have a range of flexible powers to deal adequately with pensions.

1.2   The purpose of this chapter is to trace the development of the law until its present state. This is of more than historical interest because little, with the exception of *Brooks v Brooks* (as to which see **1.12**), of substance has been repealed by the new Act; the various attempts of the courts and of Parliament to provide a means of taking pensions into account remain good law, and the law on this topic can best be described as a cumulative series of options, all of which are available to the court in appropriate circumstances.

1.3   The essential stages through which this process has gone are the treatment of pensions as a resource, variation of settlement, earmarking, and finally pension sharing. They will all be considered in turn.

PENSIONS AS A RESOURCE (OFFSETTING)

1.4   Before the amendments to MCA 1973 effected by the Pensions
Act 1995,[1] the only specific provision in MCA 1973 requiring the
court to take account of pensions was s 25(2)(h), which directed the
court to have regard to:

> '. . . the value to each of the parties to the marriage of any benefit [for
> example, a pension] which, by reason of the dissolution or annul-
> ment of the marriage, that party will lose the chance of acquiring.'

However, this provision had to be read with s 25(2)(a) which directed
the court to have regard to:

> '. . . property and other financial resources which each of the parties
> to the marriage has or is likely to have in the foreseeable future.'

It was recognised that pension entitlements were such a resource.
The court was therefore required to consider the value of any pension
of either party and to bear that in mind when making its final order. It
is fair to say, however, that in most cases pensions did not figure
prominently as a decisive issue, and the words 'in the foreseeable
future' caused the courts to regard the relevance of pensions as
somewhat limited.[2]

1.5   The emphasis changed with the enactment of the Pensions Act
1995 and the new sections which it introduced into MCA 1973. As will
be seen below, this included the concept of 'earmarking', but
amendments were also made to s 25 of MCA 1973 to change the
emphasis in relation to the consideration of pensions. Section
25(2)(h) was amended to delete the words '(for example, a pension)'
and s 25(2)(a) was thenceforth to be read as though there had been
removed the words 'in the foreseeable future' in any consideration of
pensions as a resource.[3] The effect of these changes, which survive
WRPA 1999, is that the court is required to have regard to the value of
any pension, no matter how far distant.

---

1   Section 166.
2   See eg *H v H (Financial Provision: Capital Allowance)* [1993] 2 FLR 335, CA,
      and *Hedges v Hedges* [1991] 1 FLR 196, CA.
3   MCA 1973, s 25B(1).

1.6 Having established that there are benefits to which the court must have regard, the court is then directed as to what it should consider. It is provided that:

> '... the court shall, in addition to considering any other matter which it is required to consider apart from this subsection, consider –
>
> (a) whether, having regard to any matter to which it is required to have regard in the proceedings by virtue of subsection (1) above, such an order (whether deferred or not) should be made, and
> (b) where the court determines to make such an order, how the terms of the order should be affected, having regard to any such matter.'[1]

In this provision, subs (1) is that which directs the court as indicated at **1.4** above, and 'such an order' refers to s 23.

1.7 The method of valuation of pension benefits is prescribed by MCA 1973 and the Regulations.[2] In effect, the pension provider must provide a cash equivalent transfer value (CETV) which the court must use as the basis of valuation; the CETV is not necessarily the last word on the subject but the court must take account of it.

Having made a finding as to the value of the pension, the court must decide what to do with it, and this is a topic which is considered in more detail in Chapter 7. Here, it may be said that the conventional approach has been to allow the person entitled to the pension to retain all its benefits and to make additional provision for the other party from any remaining assets by, for example, giving her a larger share of the proceeds of any matrimonial home. This was clearly a somewhat approximate approach, and its defects led to, first, earmarking and then pension sharing.

---

1   MCA 1973, s 25B(2), which is repealed by Sch 4 to the 1999 Act.
2   MCA 1973, s 25D(2)(e) and the Divorce etc (Pensions) Regulations 1996, SI 1996/1676 (to be replaced by the Divorce etc (Pensions) Regulations 1999).

EARMARKING

1.8   The other major innovation of the changes introduced into
MCA 1973 by the Pensions Act 1995 and which came into force on 1
August 1996 in respect of petitions filed after 1 July 1996 was
earmarking. The detail is contained in MCA 1973, ss 25B to 25D, and
the concept is simple. An earmarking order is an order directed to
the trustees or managers of a pension fund requiring them to pay to a
party who is not the pension fund member sums which would
normally have gone to the member. It is a tool rather than a separate
head of relief. An earmarking order is made under s 23 and will be
either a periodical payments order, whether deferred or not, or a
deferred lump sum order. It is always necessary to make a specific
application for an earmarking order.[1]

Although the court *may* make an earmarking order, it is obliged to
consider making such an order whenever one party has or is likely to
have a benefit under a pension scheme.[2] The court may also order a
person entitled to a benefit to commute all or part of it.

1.9   Earmarking is therefore a method of securing payment of a
capital sum or periodic amounts. All such orders, including lump
sums, can be varied. The manner in which the court should exercise
its new powers was considered by Singer J in *T v T (Financial Relief:
Pensions)*.[3] This case should be studied for the valuable guidance
given, but one of the principal rulings is that the new provisions do
nothing to upset the court's established approach under s 25, which is
to consider all the circumstances; pension benefits are but one of the
circumstances and, while they may be prominent in certain cases,
there is nothing to give them unique prominence in every case. The
WRPA 1999 has made some changes to the detail of earmarking
orders, and these are considered in Chapter 6.

---

1   MCA 1973, s 25B(2) and (3).
2   MCA 1973, s 25B(2).
3   [1998] 1 FLR 1072.

VARIATION OF SETTLEMENTS

1.10 The achieving of a redistribution of pension rights by way of an order for variation of settlement pursuant to MCA 1973, s 24(1)(c) is a remedy which has theoretically always been possible. The court has power to vary for the benefit of a former spouse or a child 'any ante-nuptial or post-nuptial settlement . . . made on the parties to the marriage'. However, this remedy did not receive much attention until the decision of the House of Lords in *Brooks v Brooks*,[1] and, due to the limited circumstances in which it is likely to be applicable, it would have been unlikely to receive widespread attention in future, particularly after the advent of pension sharing. Nevertheless, it was to some extent regarded as a landmark decision, and must be briefly explained.

1.11 The features of the *Brooks* pension scheme which led the court to categorise it as a post-nuptial settlement were as follows:

(a)   it was set up after the marriage, and was clearly post-nuptial;
(b)   it had only one scheme member, namely the husband;
(c)   no other beneficiary was involved. Lord Nichols in his speech said that it would not be right to vary the rights of one scheme member to the detriment of other scheme members;
(d)   the wife had earnings of her own from the family company which supported a pension for her of the relevant amount;
(e)   the approval of the pension provider and the trustees of the scheme was required and was forthcoming.

The other point of the greatest importance was that the variation of the scheme approved by the court must have Inland Revenue approval.[2]

1.12 Given all these factors, the court felt able to find that the pension scheme was a post-nuptial settlement. It was also appropriate to vary it, although of course that would not necessarily follow in all cases. The only reason why it might be thought desirable to obtain a *Brooks v Brooks* order now would be that, unlike a pension sharing

---

1 [1995] 2 FLR 13, HL.
2 See Taxes Act 1988, s 590 et seq.

order, it would permit 'rebuilding' (as to which see Chapter 3 at **3.14**). However, this option is no longer available since the amended MCA 1973, s 21(2)(c) and (d) in effect exclude a marriage settlement which is in 'the form of a pension arrangement (within the meaning of section 25D ...)' from the classes of settlement which may be varied. The remedy established by *Brooks v Brooks* is, therefore, abolished by statute.

THE CASE FOR PENSION SHARING

1.13   It has been seen that by 1996 the courts were able to approach the task of recognising the importance of pensions in various ways. The pension might be regarded as a resource of one of the parties and taken into account when and if other assets of the parties were being redistributed. The duty of the court to take account of pensions was reinforced by the 1995 amendments to MCA 1973. In certain limited circumstances, the pension might be regarded as an ante or post-nuptial settlement and varied in appropriate terms. Finally, earmarking orders as to income or capital or both could be made, ensuring that sums due to the pension scheme member would be paid direct to the non-member.

1.14   However, the law was still regarded by many as unsatisfactory. Merely to treat pensions as a resource was a somewhat approximate way of doing justice between the parties, and an earmarking order meant that there could not be a complete clean break. Earmarking also suffered from the fact that, if the pension scheme member died before the other spouse and before payment, all the benefits might be lost; furthermore, earmarking orders, even of a capital nature, were subject to variation. What the critics, who were mainly concerned with the interests of women, wanted was the ability to detach from the pension a share which could then be taken away and regarded as the separate and independent pension of the non-member.

1.15   Matters came to a head during the Parliamentary passage of the Family Law Act 1996 (FLA 1996). Until then, the government of the day had declined to give any commitment as to pension sharing, citing the complications and potential difficulties involved. However, the then opposition pressed the issue to a division and the government was defeated in the House of Lords.[1] When the matter came to be considered in the House of Commons, the government withdrew its opposition to the new clause[2] and what is now s 16 of FLA 1996 came into being. This established the principle of pension sharing but gave the Lord Chancellor extensive powers to make regulations, extending even to the power to amend primary legislation. It was made clear that the position was far from satisfactory and that further primary legislation would be required.[3]

1.16 In July 1996, the government published a Consultation Paper 'The Treatment of Pension Rights on Divorce'[4] seeking views on a wide range of issues. After the change of government in May 1997, there was no perceptible change of pace, and a further Consultation Paper 'Pension sharing on divorce: reforming pensions for a fairer future', with draft legislation annexed, was published in June 1998. After further consultation, and some modifications of the draft legislation, the Welfare Reform and Pensions Bill was published in February 1999.

1.17 The provisions relating to pension sharing are contained in Parts III and IV of and Schs 3 to 6 to what is now WRPA 1999. The remainder of the 1999 Act relates to other changes to welfare benefits which proved controversial when the Bill was going through Parliament. By contrast, the pension sharing provisions attracted little attention and proved relatively uncontroversial except in relation to FLA 1996. It was the government's intention that pension sharing would come into force at the same time as Part II of WRPA 1996, and the Bill, including amendments to MCA 1973, was prepared on that basis. Accordingly, for example, it was proposed that an application for a pension sharing order could be made only after the filing of a statement of marital breakdown, and no order could take effect before the making of a divorce order or decree of nullity. This had to

---

1　See Official Report (HL) 29 February 1996.
2　Perhaps, in view of its narrow majority, as part of the price for securing the passage of the Bill.
3　Official Report (HL) 27 June 1996, col 1090.
4　Cm 3345.

change when, on 17 June 1999, the Lord Chancellor announced that the government did not intend to bring FLA 1996 into effect during 2000 as had been previously intended. This meant that the previously existing law and procedure of divorce would continue in the foreseeable future and so amendments had to be introduced to fit the pension sharing provisions into the existing law. Details of this process are contained in Chapter 2 at **2.12** et seq.

THE WELFARE REFORM AND PENSIONS ACT 1999

1.18 The law on pension sharing is now contained in Parts III to IV and Schs 3 to 6 and 12 of WRPA 1999. Part IV brings about the changes to MCA 1973 contained in Sch 3; in addition to providing for pension sharing, the provisions as to earmarking etc contained in ss 25B to 25D of MCA 1973 are amended to take account of the introduction of pension sharing. Part III of the Matrimonial and Family Proceedings Act 1984 (MFPA 1984) (financial relief after overseas divorce etc) is also amended to introduce corresponding provisions. Part IV contains the detail of pension sharing, both in relation to State pensions and 'private' pensions. Schedule 3 contains the amendments to MCA 1973 which confer new powers on the court and Sch 4 contains certain consequential amendments. Schedule 5 deals with the mode of discharge of pension credits, and Sch 6 with the effect of State scheme debits and credits. Finally, Sch 12 contains the amendments to FLA 1996 including the amendments to MCA 1973 which will be effected when Part II of FLA 1996 comes into force.

1.19 In conclusion, two fundamental points should be noted.

(1)   Pension sharing is a new option which is added to the court's existing range of powers; it does not replace earmarking which remains available, and the court is not directed to prefer pension sharing over any other remedy.

(2) Pension sharing is available only to those people who begin proceedings for divorce or nullity after WRPA 1999 has been brought into force; that will be a day to be determined by the Lord Chancellor and seems unlikely to be earlier than 2001. This might lead a pension scheme member who wished to prevent pension sharing to present a petition before the appointed day. Whether or not this stratagem would succeed, however, may be open to doubt. There seems to be no reason why the other party should not present his or her own petition after the appointed day (provided the marriage had not yet been dissolved or annulled); the court would then have to give directions as to how the two petitions were to proceed. However, there seems to be no clear authority on this point.

Chapter 2

WHAT IS PENSION SHARING?

INTRODUCTION

2.1   With the enactment of WRPA 1999, pension sharing is now part of the law of ancillary relief. The purpose of this chapter will be to examine the basic principles of pension sharing and the process which has been created by the 1999 Act. The effect of pension sharing will then be considered in the next chapter.

2.2   Two important preliminary points must be made.

(1)   Pension sharing will be available only in cases where the divorce or nullity proceedings (not judicial separation proceedings) were commenced after WRPA 1999 comes into force. Although the Act has received Royal Assent, pension sharing is contained in Parts III and IV and Schs 3 to 6 to the Act, which are not due to come into force until a day to be appointed by the Lord Chancellor; it is thought that this will be in 2001.

(2)   With the exception of *Brooks v Brooks*, pension sharing does not replace the existing powers of the court in respect of pensions; some of these have been amended by WRPA 1999, but they remain in force as part of a package of remedies which has been extended by the arrival of pension sharing.

2.3   This point was made clear in the Parliamentary debates, in the course of which a government spokesperson said that:

'Pensions are already part of the financial settlements on divorce ... they can be offset against other assets or earmarked currently. What we are doing, and what the House was persuaded to say to the other House, was that pension sharing was an additional choice to couples and to the courts in seeking to achieve the fairest disposition of assets at the point of a marriage break up, and the financial settlement with divorce. It may not always be the right solution. Offsetting, or earmarking may be more appropriate. Nor do we say that the division has to be 50:50; it can be 10 per cent or 90 per cent depending on the family circumstances.'[1]

TO WHAT DOES PENSION SHARING APPLY?

2.4   When pension sharing was being advocated as a solution to the injustice suffered by (mainly) former wives, the impression was given that this would provide a simple and effective means of resolving pensions disputes in most cases. The reality is a little more complicated. The basic principle is that 'pension sharing is available under this Chapter (Ch I of Part IV of WRPA 1999) in relation to a person's shareable rights under any pension arrangement other than an excepted public service pension scheme.'[2] A person's shareable rights under a pension arrangement are 'any rights of his under the arrangement' other than rights of a description specified by regulations made by the Secretary of State for Social Security.[3] It is intended that such regulations will specify and therefore exclude from pension sharing survivors' benefits payable to a pension scheme member in his capacity as a survivor, an injury benefit, a compensation payment and incidental payments such as travel concessions. Subject to those limited exceptions, most pension rights will be shareable. As to the 'excepted public service pension scheme', it is provided that a scheme is excepted if specified by the appropriate Minister or government department,[4] and it is intended to use this power to except the 'Great offices of State', that is to say the offices of Prime Minister, Lord Chancellor and Speaker.[5]

2.5   'Pension arrangement' is defined as:

'(a)   an occupational pension scheme,
(b)   a personal pension scheme,

---

1   Baroness Hollis, Official Report (HL) 6 July 1999, col 776.
2   WRPA 1999, s 27(1).
3   WRPA 1999, s 27(2).
4   WRPA 1999, s 27(3).
5   The reason being that pensions in respect of such offices become payable immediately the holder leaves that office, and not at a future retirement age.

(c)   a retirement annuity contract,

(d)   an annuity or insurance policy purchased, or transferred, for the purpose of giving effect to rights under an occupational pension scheme or a personal pension scheme, and

(e)   an annuity purchased, or entered into, for the purpose of discharging liability in respect of a credit under section 29(1)(b) or under corresponding Northern Ireland legislation;'[1].

'Occupational pension scheme' and 'personal pension scheme' are defined as having the meanings attributed to them by s 1 of the Pension Schemes Act 1993 (PSA 1993); 'retirement annuity contract' means a contract approved under Ch III of Part XIV of the Income and Corporation Taxes Act 1988 (ICTA 1988).[2]

2.6   The effect of all this is, therefore, that provided a person has rights in a pension arrangement of the kind set out at **2.4**, and neither of the two limited exceptions set out at **2.3** applies, those rights are 'shareable'. Pension sharing will, therefore, be available in most cases.

SHARING OF STATE SCHEME RIGHTS

2.7   To avoid any confusion, the sharing of State scheme rights (ie additional retirement pension), and its effect, are dealt with separately in Chapter 4.

WHAT IS A PENSION SHARING ORDER?

2.8   Before going on to consider the timing of pension sharing orders, it may be convenient to consider what a pension sharing order actually does, and how it is to be expressed.

2.9   It is provided that a pension sharing order is:

---

1   WRPA 1999, s 46(1).
2   WRPA 1999, s 46(1).

'... an order which –

(a)   provides that one party's –
         (i)   shareable rights under a specified pension arrange-
                  ment, or
         (ii)   shareable state scheme rights,
         be subject to pension sharing for the benefit of the other
         party, and
(b)   specifies the percentage value to be transferred.'[1]

The essentials of the order are therefore that one party's shareable rights are subject to pension sharing for the benefit of the other party; the reference to 'a specified pension arrangement' means merely that the pension arrangement must be named in the order. The order, in effect, transfers rights to the other party, and it must specify the 'percentage value' to be transferred.

2.10 The order may, therefore, apply to two kinds of pension schemes:

(1)   a specified pension arrangement; and
(2)   a State scheme.

The first category will be a pension arrangement of the kind set out at **2.3** above. Shareable State schemes are defined in WRPA 1999, s 47(2), and are limited to entitlement or prospective entitlement to a Category A retirement pension by virtue of s 44(3)(b) of the Social Security Contributions and Benefits Act 1992 (earnings-related additional pension) or under s 55A of the 1992 Act (shared additional pension).

2.11 The Act refers to 'one or more' pension sharing orders. As will be seen below, the Bill was originally prepared on the assumption that it would come into force at the same time as FLA 1996, and it was to be provided that:

'the court shall exercise its powers under this section, so far as is practicable, by making on one occasion all such provision as can be

---

1   MCA 1973, s 21A(1) (inserted by WRPA 1999, Sch 3).

made by way of one or more pension sharing orders in relation to the marriage as it thinks fit.'

That provision still exists in respect of the position as it will be when the 1996 Act comes into force.[1] As to the position under MCA 1973 before FLA 1996 comes into force, it may be said that the reference to 'one or more' orders is similar to the jurisdiction to make an order for payment of 'such lump sum or sums' contained in the unamended MCA 1973.[2] It has been held that that refers to the power to order several lump sums on the same occasion rather than to more than one order at different times.[3] It seems, however, that the intention of this provision is to make it possible to apply for different pension sharing orders against different pension arrangements at different times.

WHEN MAY PENSION SHARING OCCUR?

2.12 The Bill was originally drafted on the basis that it would come into force at the same time as FLA 1996, Part II, and that it would dovetail with the new regime for divorce and ancillary relief to be established by the 1996 Act. This was not to be; on 17 June 1999 the Lord Chancellor announced that he did not intend to implement Part II in the year 2000 as had been planned, and the resulting position was clearly set out by the government spokesperson in the House of Lords on 6 July 1999 as follows:

'The decision to delay implementation of Part II of the Family Law Act beyond 2000 has a significant consequence for the pension sharing provisions in this Bill. The pension sharing provisions in the Bill are currently drafted on the basis that the Family Law Act will have been implemented. That is why mention is made of the statement of marital breakdown and the period of reflection and consideration, for example, which are created by Part II of the FLA. However, we can no longer assume that the new divorce process set out in the FLA will be implemented before we are ready to bring the pension sharing provisions into force, which we want to do as soon as

---

1   FLA 1996, Sch 2, para 6A as amended by WRPA 1999, Sch 12, para 65(9) (amending MCA 1973, s 24B).

2   Section 23(1)(c).

3   *Coleman v Coleman* [1973] Fam 10.

possible. Therefore we must change the Bill almost belt and braces style so that pension sharing can be made available under today's divorce law as well as under the new procedures that would be established by the FLA – otherwise the one would depend on the other and we would push pension sharing into the long grass.'[1]

2.13 What follows summarises the position as it will be when WRPA 1999 comes into force. However, the reader who wishes to consult the Act itself may be helped by understanding that Part IV contains the law as it will be before the coming into force of FLA 1996, and brings about the amendments to MCA 1973 contained in Sch 3, although s 25(1)(b) and (c) and (2) will be relevant only when FLA 1996 comes into force. Schedule 12, paras 64 to 66 to WRPA 1999, amend FLA 1996 and will come into force only when Part II of that Act comes into force; as part of the amendments, the amended FLA 1996 will introduce new ss 24B, 24BA, 24BB and 24BC of MCA 1973 and the now new s 24B of MCA 1973 introduced by Sch 3 will then be replaced by those provisions.

2.14 In considering the question of when a pension sharing order may be made, therefore, it is necessary to distinguish between the position as it will be after WRPA 1999 comes into force but before Part II of FLA 1996 comes into force, and the position as it will be after FLA 1996 comes into force. These two scenarios will be considered in turn. First, however, s 28(1) of WRPA 1999 may be considered since it covers both positions. It is provided that s 29 applies (ie debits and credits are created and pension sharing is activated) on the taking effect of any of the following:

'(a) a pension sharing order under the Matrimonial Causes Act 1973,
(b) provision which corresponds to the provision which may be made by such an order and which –
  (i) is contained in a qualifying agreement between the parties to a marriage, and
  (ii) takes effect on the dissolution of the marriage under the Family Law Act 1996,
(c) provision which corresponds to the provision which may be made by such an order and which –

---

1   Baroness Hollis, Official Report (HL) 6 July 1999, col 781.

(i) is contained in a qualifying agreement between the parties to a marriage or former marriage, and

(iii) takes effect after the dissolution of the marriage under the Family Law Act 1996,

(d) an order under Part III of the Matrimonial and Family Proceedings Act 1984 ... corresponding to such order as is mentioned in paragraph (a),'.[1]

2.15 From this, it will be seen that only (a) and (d) apply before the coming into force of Part II of FLA 1996. The remainder must await that event.

THE POSITION BEFORE PART II OF FLA 1996 COMES INTO FORCE

2.16 Once WRPA 1999 is in force, and before Part II of FLA 1996 is in force, pension sharing will be dependent on a court order, and the court will have the same jurisdiction to make a pension sharing order as for any other financial provision order, namely 'on granting a decree of divorce or a decree of nullity of marriage or at any time thereafter (whether before or after the decree is made absolute)'.[2] It is further provided that a pension sharing order 'is not to take effect unless the decree on or after which it is made has been made absolute'.[3] The position is therefore clear; there has to be a decree nisi of divorce or a decree of nullity before the order may be made, and it may not take effect until decree absolute. A pension sharing order may not be made after a decree of judicial separation, and no agreement can bring about pension sharing unless it forms the basis of a consent order. The position as to orders made after overseas divorce etc is considered at **2.12**.

2.17 There are certain further restrictions on the taking effect of such order. No pension sharing order may be made so as to take effect before the end of such period after the making of the order as

---

1   WRPA 1999, s 28(1).
2   MCA 1973, s 24B(1), as amended by WRPA 1999, Sch 3, para 4.
3   MCA 1973, s 24B(2).

may be prescribed by regulations to be made by the Lord Chancellor.[1] It is thought that such rules will require any order to be stayed until the end of the period for giving notice of appeal and that, if notice of appeal is given within that period, the order will be further stayed until the proceedings on appeal have come to an end.

2.18 The Act also imposes a separate set of restrictions which, in effect, prevent a pension sharing order in respect of a pension arrangement which is already subject to such an order in respect of that marriage. No pension sharing order may be made

> '… in relation to a pension arrangement which –
>
> (a) is the subject of a pension sharing order in relation to the marriage, or
> (b) has been the subject of pension sharing between the parties to the marriage.'[2]

The intention of the distinction between (a) and (b) is that the former is intended to relate to a previous order which has not yet taken effect, and the latter to an order (or, after Part II of FLA 1996 comes into force, an agreement) which has been made and which has taken effect. Other issues arising out of this provision are discussed at **7.9**.

2.19 There are similar restrictions in respect of shareable State scheme rights, and an identical formula to that set out at **2.13** is used to prevent a pension sharing order being made in relation to such rights.[3]

2.20 It is finally provided that a pension sharing order may not be made in relation to the rights of a person under a pension arrangement if there is in force a requirement imposed by virtue of ss 25B or 25C which relate to benefits or future benefits to which he is entitled under the pension arrangement.[4] Therefore, if an ear-

---

1   MCA 1973, s 24C(1) as amended by WRPA 1999, Sch 3.
2   MCA 1973, s 24B(3).
3   MCA 1973, s 24B(4).
4   MCA 1973, s 24B(5).

marking or attachment order has been made under ss 25B or 25C, no further order may be made and pension sharing would not be available in respect of that pension arrangement. Furthermore, this provision is not qualified by the words 'in relation to the marriage', and it would seem therefore that an order made in respect of a previous marriage would prevent the making of any further order in respect of that pension arrangement.

PENSION SHARING ORDERS AFTER OVERSEAS DIVORCE

2.21   Part III of MFPA 1984 conferred on the courts of England and Wales the power in certain circumstances to make orders for financial relief after a divorce granted in another jurisdiction. The WRPA 1999 provides that the court may, after such an overseas divorce, make an order corresponding to a pension sharing order. Section 22 contains various provisions to amend MFPA 1984 in a manner similar to the amendments of MCA 1973, and also introduces ss 25B and 25C of MCA 1973 into MFPA 1984, with the effect that the powers of the court under MFPA 1984 are now identical with those under MCA 1973. The restrictions mentioned at **2.17–2.20** apply equally to orders made under MFPA 1984.

THE POSITION AFTER PART II OF FLA 1996 COMES INTO FORCE

2.22   Once Part II of FLA 1996 is in force, pension sharing may occur as a result of either a court order or an agreement (see **2.14**). The significance of court orders is clear enough, and will be discussed below, particularly with reference to the timing thereof. When agreements are discussed, it will be seen that there are significant restrictions on the kind of agreements which are capable of creating an enforceable pension sharing arrangement.

PENSION SHARING BY COURT ORDER DURING OR AFTER DIVORCE PROCEEDINGS

2.23 There will be three types of court order which may give rise to pension sharing. The first, and by far the most common, will be an order in the course of, or after, proceedings for divorce. The second is an order made on or after the grant of a decree of nullity. The third is an order made after the grant of an overseas divorce and in this respect, at least, the position will not change under FLA 1996. The first two types of order will be considered in turn.

2.24 The amendments to FLA 1996 effected by WRPA 1999[1] insert into MCA 1973 a new s 24B, which provides that:

> '(1) On an application made under this section, the court may at the appropriate time make one or more pension sharing orders.'

This is the jurisdiction for any pension sharing order made in divorce proceedings under Part II of FLA 1996.

2.25 Section 24B goes on to define 'the appropriate time'. The definition will be familiar to divorce practitioners acquainted with FLA 1996 since it is in most respects identical to the definition contained elsewhere in the post FLA 1996, Part II amendment of MCA 1973 of the appropriate time for making any orders for ancillary relief; the difference is that, with one exception, references to separation are omitted. The appropriate time for the making of a pension sharing order is any time:

(a) after a statement of marital breakdown has been received by the court and before any application for a divorce order or for a separation order is made to the court by reference to that statement;

(b) when an application for a divorce order has been made under s 3 of FLA 1996 and has not been withdrawn;

(c) when an application for a divorce order has been made under s 4 of FLA 1996 and has not been withdrawn;

---

1   See WRPA 1999, Sch 12, para 65(9).

(d)   after a divorce order has been made.[1]

The appropriate time is therefore the same as for any other ancillary relief order made in divorce proceedings. The reference to 'a separation order' in (a) above seems otiose, as no pensions sharing order may take effect before the making of a divorce order.

2.26   As to the reference to 'one or more' pension sharing orders, this is the same formula adopted by MCA 1973 as amended by FLA 1996 in respect of other orders for ancillary relief, and, as elsewhere, it is provided here that:

> 'The court shall exercise its powers under this section, so far as is practicable, by making on one occasion all such provision as can be made by way of one or more pension sharing orders in relation to the marriage as it thinks fit.'[2]

There are certain further restrictions on the making of pension sharing orders, which are similar to those applicable to any order for ancillary relief under the regime established by FLA 1996. No such order may be made so as to take effect before the making of a divorce order in relation to the marriage.[3] This is of particular relevance because, under FLA 1996 procedure, parties will be permitted, even expected, to obtain their orders for ancillary relief during the period for reflection and consideration. No order may be made at any time while the period for reflection and consideration is interrupted under s 7(8) of FLA 1996.[4] No such order may be made by virtue of a statement of marital breakdown if, by virtue of s 5(3) or s 7(9) (lapse of divorce process), it has ceased to be possible for an application for a divorce order to be made or for an order to be made on such an application.[5] Finally, no order may be made after a divorce order has been made except in response to an application made before the divorce order was made or with leave of the court.[6] In addition to

---

1   MCA 1973, s 24B(2) as amended by WRPA 1999, Sch 12.
2   MCA 1973, s 24B(3).
3   MCA 1973, s 24BA(1).
4   MCA 1973, s 24BA(2).
5   MCA 1973, s 24BA(3).
6   MCA 1973, s 24BA(4).

these restrictions, which depend on the coming into force of Part II of FLA 1996, the same restrictions applicable before FLA 1996, Part II, as set out at **2.17–2.20** will be applicable.[1]

PENSION SHARING BY COURT ORDER ON OR AFTER DECREE OF NULLITY

2.27   It is provided that on or after granting a decree of nullity of marriage (whether before or after the decree is made absolute) the court may, on an application made under the new s 24BB of MCA 1973, make one or more pension sharing orders in relation to the marriage.[2] The only distinction to bear in mind is that, as nullity proceedings are not affected by FLA 1996, the time for making such orders is that familiar under the pre-FLA procedure, namely on or after the grant of decree, and the formula of 'the appropriate time' is not applicable. The order could not take effect until decree absolute.[3]

2.28   Although WRPA 1999 refers to 'one or more' orders, it is also provided that the court must exercise its powers, so far as is practicable, by making on one occasion all such provision as can be made by way of one or more pension sharing orders in relation to the marriage as it thinks fit.[4] There are also restrictions in the case of orders in nullity cases which are identical with those set out at **2.17–2.20**.

PENSION SHARING BY AGREEMENT

2.29   The second broad category of events which may activate pension sharing is those where an agreement has been made. However, not any agreement will suffice; as will be seen, the only

---

1   See MCA 1973, s 24BA(5) to (7) .
2   MCA 1973, s 24BB as amended by WRPA 1999, Sch 12, para 65(9).
3   MCA 1973, s 24BB(3).
4   MCA 1973, s 24BB(2).

agreements which will be sufficient to activate pension sharing are those which the parties have made in order to resolve the financial issues between them in proceedings for divorce or nullity. The agreements which may be may be eligible fall into two classes, namely qualifying agreements:

(a)   which are effective on the dissolution of the marriage;
(b)   which are effective after dissolution of marriage.[1]

These will all be considered in turn. However, first two further essential conditions applicable to all cases must be considered.

2.30   The first condition is that the provision made by the agreement must correspond to the provision which may be made by a pension sharing order.[2] In other words, all the conditions relating to orders which were set out above must be met if the agreement is to be recognised. The second condition is that the agreement must be a 'qualifying agreement'.[3] This is defined as one which:

(a)   has been entered into in such circumstances as the Lord Chancellor may prescribe by regulations; and
(b)   satisfies such requirements as the Lord Chancellor may so prescribe.[4]

As to the circumstances into which an agreement was entered into, it seems that regulations may prescribe two requirements. First, the regulations will require that the parties have given prior notice to the person responsible for the pension arrangement of their intention to pension share. Secondly, the agreement must have been reached following mediation or other form of negotiation involving a third party. This second requirement accords with the definition of 'negotiated agreement' in FLA 1996, s 9(2)(b) and Sch 1, para 7. Production of a negotiated agreement is one of the ways in which the parties may satisfy the court that all necessary arrangements for the future have been made, and it seems to be the case that, for example,

---

1   See WRPA 1999, s 28(1)(b)(ii) and (c)(ii).
2   WRPA 1999, s 28(1)(b) and (c).
3   WRPA 1999, s 28(1)(b)(i) and (c)(i).
4   WRPA 1999, s 28(2).

an agreement negotiated between solicitors would not suffice; the involvement of some mediator or neutral third party would seem to be necessary.

2.31 As to the prescribed requirements, it is thought that the Lord Chancellor intends to prescribe that agreements must meet requirements as to form, contain prescribed information, and must have been produced to the court before being passed on to the pension arrangement concerned. These details will all be contained in the regulations.

2.32 Having established that the conditions as set out above are met, there will therefore be two types of agreement which may activate pension sharing. The first is an agreement which:

(a)   is contained in a qualifying agreement between the parties to a marriage; and
(b)   takes effect on the dissolution of the marriage under FLA 1996.

The two essential points are first that it is made between the parties to a marriage, so that the marriage has not yet been dissolved, and that the agreement (or rather, its terms as to pension sharing) are to take effect on the dissolution of the marriage (ie as soon as a divorce order is granted). This is the kind of agreement which will be made by parties in contemplation of divorce and as part of their arrangements for the future.

2.33 This class of agreement will be subject to certain restrictions. It is provided that WRPA 1999, s 28(1)(b) does not apply (ie such an agreement will not activate pension sharing) in two sets of circumstances. The first is when:

> 'the pension arrangement to which the provision relates is the subject of a pension sharing order under the Matrimonial Causes Act 1973 in relation to the marriage.'[1]

'The marriage' means the marriage between these parties. If there is a pension sharing order made in proceedings between them and

---

1   WRPA 1999, s 28(4)(a).

affecting the pension arrangement which it is intended to affect by the agreement, the agreement will be of no effect.

2.34 The second restriction is that WRPA 1999, s 28(1)(b) does not apply when:

> 'there is in force a requirement imposed by virtue of section 25B or 25C of [MCA 1973] ... which relates to benefits or future benefits to which the party who is the transferor is entitled under the pension arrangement to which the provision relates.'[1]

The powers of the court under s 25B and s 25C of MCA 1973 were discussed at **1.8** et seq, and relate to orders for earmarking, commutation and so on. If, therefore, an order has been made under those provisions, the parties are precluded from making any agreement for pension sharing in respect of that pension arrangement.

2.35 As has been seen, the second type of agreement which may activate pension sharing will be one which:

(a)   is contained in a qualifying agreement between the parties to a marriage or former marriage; and

(b)   takes effect after the dissolution of the marriage under FLA 1996.

In these cases, therefore, the divorce may or may not have been granted. The parties may be still going through the divorce process, or may have been divorced for any length of time. The essential point is that the pension sharing is not to be activated until after the dissolution of the marriage. The reason for establishing this as a separate category is that, in order to obtain their divorce in the first place, the parties will have had to satisfy the court as to their future arrangements, and this therefore has an effect on the restrictions which are placed on this kind of agreement.

2.36 It is therefore provided that this subsection does not apply (ie the agreement will not activate pension sharing) in three sets of circumstances. The first is when:

---

1   WRPA 1999, s 28(4)(b).

'the marriage was dissolved by an order under section 3 of the Family Law Act 1996 (divorce not preceded by separation) and the satisfaction of the requirements of section 9(2) of that Act (settlement of future financial arrangements) was a precondition to the making of the order,'.[1]

The meaning of the first set of words in parenthesis may give rise to some doubt, but the intention of this provision is thought to be that parties who obtain a divorce on the strength of their assurance to the court that they have settled their future financial arrangements in one of the ways prescribed by s 9(2) of FLA 1976 are thereby precluded from making further arrangements as to pensions by a subsequent agreement. Agreements or arrangements under s 9(2) are, therefore, to be taken seriously.

2.37 The second set of circumstances is that the pension arrangement to which the provision relates:

(a)   is the subject of a pension sharing order under MCA 1973 in relation to the marriage; or

(b)   has already been the subject of pension sharing between the parties.[2]

This reinforces the general principle that pension sharing may only occur once.

The third set of circumstances is identical to s 28(4)(b), namely that the pension arrangement is subject to an order made under s 25B or s 25C of MCA 1973.

CONCLUSION

2.38 It is hoped that this chapter has made clear the somewhat tangled threads governing the circumstances in which pension sharing may occur. Clearly, the position will change if Part II of FLA 1996 is ever introduced. The reader may gain comfort in the

---

1   WRPA 1999, s 28(5)(a).
2   WRPA 1999, s 28(5)(b).

knowledge that, at least, when pension sharing is first introduced, it will be in the context of a system of divorce and ancillary relief which is familiar.

Chapter 3

THE EFFECT OF PENSION SHARING

INTRODUCTION

3.1 It was seen in Chapter 2 that a pension sharing order is one which provides that one party's shareable rights under a specified pension arrangement or shareable State scheme rights are subject to pension sharing for the benefit of the other party and specifies the percentage value to be transferred; such an order will, therefore, always transfer to the other party a percentage of the shareable rights (unlike the position in Scotland, where it is possible to transfer a stated value of the pension arrangement). When, after the coming into force of Part II of FLA 1996, it is possible for pension sharing to be effected by certain agreements, an agreement for pension sharing will be valid only if it corresponds to the provision which a court would order. In this chapter, it is intended to consider what this actually means. What will be the effect for the parties, and for the providers of the pension arrangement? This chapter relates to pensions which are not State scheme pensions. The latter are dealt with at Chapter 4.

DEBITS AND CREDITS

3.2 The creation of pension debits and credits is at the heart of pension sharing. It is provided that 'on the application of this section', ie on the making of a pension sharing order or the making of an agreement which activates pension sharing:

> '(a) the transferor's shareable rights under the relevant arrangement become subject to a debit of the appropriate amount, and

(b) the transferee becomes entitled to a credit of that amount as against the person responsible for that arrangement.'[1]

The transferor therefore loses the percentage required to be transferred, so that his pension fund is reduced in value, and the transferee acquires the right to require the pension scheme trustee or manager to credit her with that amount so that she gains a pension fund of that value. The pension has been, in the terms originally envisaged for these purposes, split. The transferee now has her own pension.

HOW MUCH IS TRANSFERRED?

3.3   When, as is always the case in England and Wales, the order or provision specifies a percentage value to be transferred, what is the total amount of which a percentage is calculated? WRPA 1999 provides that this is 'the cash equivalent of the relevant benefits on the valuation day'.[2] Three points arise from this, namely the meaning of 'relevant benefits', 'valuation day' and 'cash equivalent'. These must be considered in turn.

1. Relevant benefits

3.4   What the relevant benefits will be depends, in effect, on whether or not the pension is an occupational scheme of which the transferor is an active member. In such cases, it is provided that:

> 'where the relevant arrangement is an occupational pension scheme and the transferor is in pensionable service under the scheme on the transfer day, the relevant benefits ... are the benefits or future benefits to which he would be entitled under the scheme by virtue of his shareable rights under it had his pensionable service terminated immediately before that day.'[3]

---

1   WRPA 1999, s 29(1).
2   WRPA 1999, s 29(2).
3   WRPA 1999, s 29(4).

It will be seen that there are two essential features of this definition. First, the scheme must be an occupational pension scheme as defined by s 1 of PSA 1993. Secondly, the transferor must be in pensionable service on the transfer day (ie the day on which the relevant order or provision takes effect); in other words, the transferor must be still accruing rights under the scheme. For the purposes of calculating the relevant benefits, therefore, it is assumed that the transferor ceased to be an active member the day before the order or provision took effect.

3.5   In all other cases, where these two essential features are not present, it is provided that:

> '... the relevant benefits ... are the benefits or future benefits to which, immediately before the transfer day, the transferor is entitled under the terms of the relevant arrangement by virtue of his shareable rights under it.'[1]

2. Valuation day

3.6   The cash equivalent must be valued as at 'the valuation day', which is defined as:

> 'such day within the implementation period for the credit ... as the person responsible for the relevant arrangement may specify by notice in writing to the transferor and transferee.'[2]

This provides scope for the person responsible for the pension arrangements to choose the day on which the valuation will be made, but such day must fall within the implementation period, such period being the time for compliance as stated in the order or provision (which is to be the subject of regulations).

3. Cash equivalent

3.7   The process for valuation of the cash equivalent is to be prescribed by regulations made by the Secretary of State for Social Security pursuant to s 30(1) of WRPA 1999. These regulations have

---

1   WRPA 1999, s 29(5).
2   WRPA 1999, s 29(7).

not yet been made, but the government has indicated how it proposes to approach the matter.[1] It is intended to adopt the method already in use for valuing the pension rights of 'early leavers' from occupational pension schemes or of members of personal pension schemes who wish to transfer their accrued rights to another pension scheme or arrangement. The regulations will broadly reflect the principles set out for calculating cash equivalents for early leavers. In the case of salary-related schemes, it is intended that cash equivalents should be calculated in a manner approved by a qualified actuary. In cases where members have acquired rights in public service schemes, the manner of calculation will be approved by the government actuary.

3.8 Where a salary-related occupational scheme is subject to the 'minimum funding requirement' (MFR), there will also be a requirement that the cash equivalent must be of at least a minimum amount, consistent with the methods and assumptions used for calculating the MFR adjusted, where appropriate, to take account of the fact that a cash equivalent for pension sharing is made on an individual and not a collective basis.

Where the cash equivalent relates to salary-related benefits, it will normally be calculated and verified in a manner approved by the scheme actuary; the Secretary of State intends to discuss the formulae with the professional bodies.

THE EFFECT ON THE TRANSFEROR

1. Reduction of transferor's benefits

3.9 The question which must now be addressed is what is the effect on the pension entitlement of the transferor of the pension sharing order or agreement. The general rule, contained in s 31(1) of WRPA 1999, is that, where a person's shareable rights under a pension arrangement are subject to a pension debit:

---

1   See, generally, Explanatory Notes to WRPA 1999 (available from The Stationery Office Limited and not reproduced in this book).

'... each benefit or future benefit –

(a) to which he is entitled under the arrangement by virtue of those rights, and

(b) which is a qualifying benefit,

is reduced by the appropriate percentage.'

However, this is subject to s 31(2) of WRPA 1999, which applies when the pension debit relates to the shareable rights under an occupational pension scheme of a person who is in pensionable service under the scheme on the transfer day. In such cases, each benefit or future benefit:

'(a) to which the person is entitled under the scheme by virtue of those rights, and

(b) which corresponds to a qualifying benefit,

is reduced by an amount equal to the appropriate percentage of the corresponding qualifying benefit.'

Whether or not a benefit is a 'qualifying benefit' for the purpose of these provisions depends on whether the cash equivalent by reference to which the amount of the pension debit is determined includes an amount in respect of it.[1]

3.10 It is possible to give examples of how this will work in practice.[2] Taking the formula in subs (1) above, which applies to all cases except serving members of occupational pension schemes, the debit will be a once and for all reduction of a percentage of the accrued value of the fund. If the cash equivalent is, say, £100,000 and 40% is to be transferred, the transferor will be left with a fund worth £60,000. Each qualifying benefit must be reduced in the same proportion. For example, if a deferred member of a contracted-out salary-related scheme (COSR) had both guaranteed minimum pension (GMP) rights and rights in excess of GMP, and 40% of the member's cash equivalent was debited, both the GMP rights and the rights in excess of GMP would suffer a deduction of 40%.

---

1   WRPA 1999, s 31(3).
2   Taken from Explanatory Notes to WRPA 1999.

3.11 This must be contrasted with the position under subs (2), which deals with the case of an active member of an occupational pension scheme who is in pensionable service on the day the order or agreement takes effect. Here, the position is more complicated, and his benefit is not simply reduced by the appropriate percentage. Instead, the benefit is reduced by an amount representing the appropriate percentage of the benefit that was taken for the purpose of calculating the cash equivalent, and that calculation is done by reference to the hypothetical deferred pension to which he would have been entitled had he retired. The benefits which are reduced are those which correspond to the benefits to which the member would have been entitled under the hypothetical pension. Thus, death in service benefit will not be reduced because such benefit does not form part of the hypothetical pension.

Example

Assume that a member of a salary-related occupational scheme with 20 years' membership at the date of the order or agreement earns £30,000 per annum. The scheme provides $\frac{1}{60}$th of final salary for each year of service. The deferred pension at the date of the order will be $\frac{20}{60} \times £30,000 = £10,000$.

Assume that the scheme actuary calculates the cash equivalent for pension sharing as £100,000 and that the pension debit ordered by the court is 40%. £40,000 will be transferred to the transferee. At retirement, the adjustment to the transferor's salary benefit will be calculated as follows. Assume he retires at 60 after 30 years' service with a final salary of £48,000. His full pension entitlement, ignoring the debit, would have been $\frac{30}{60} \times £48,000 = £24,000$. Using the statutory Revaluation Order, the scheme actuary has to calculate the equivalent value at retirement of the deferred pension given up by the transfer; this is known as 'the negative deferred pension'. That figure was £4,000 (40% × £10,000) and, for the purposes of this example, it may be assumed that at retirement the equivalent figure is £6,000 per annum. The member's pension will be reduced by that figure, leaving £18,000. The use of this formula is intended to prevent the scheme from enjoying a windfall at the member's expense.

2. The effect on contracted-out rights

3.12 Section 32 of WRPA 1999 makes certain amendments to PSA 1993 to provide for the effect of pension sharing on the contracted-out rights of a transferor. Since this is a topic which is unlikely to involve family lawyers in litigation, the provisions will be summarised rather than set out in detail. The background to these provisions is the right of a member of certain occupational pension schemes to contract out of the State earnings-related pension scheme (SERPS) and, as a result, to pay reduced National Insurance contributions. Before 6 April 1997, contracted-out salary-related schemes (COSR) had to provide a guaranteed minimum pension (GMP) roughly equivalent to SERPS. Following changes introduced by the Pensions Act 1995 (PA 1995), such schemes are no longer required to pay a GMP for pensionable service from 6 April 1997. Instead, they must meet an overall quality test and a minimum funding requirement, and pensions in payment derived from post 6 April 1997 service must also rise by at least 5% per annum or in line with prices, whichever is the lower.

Protected rights are the rights in a contracted-out money purchase scheme (COMP) and appropriate personal pension schemes (APP) which derive from the rebate of National Insurance contributions and, in APP schemes only, tax relief on the employee's share of the rebate.

3. The effect of amendments to PSA 1993

3.13 With this background in mind, the effect of the amendments to PSA 1993 brought about by s 32 of WRPA 1999 may be summarised as follows.

(1) Protected rights in a COMP or an APP which is subject to a pension sharing debit are reduced by the percentage specified in the order or agreement.

(2) A GMP payable by a COSR scheme is reduced where it is subject to a pension debit. For example, if the cash equivalent has been reduced by 40%, the GMP accrued at the date the order or agreement takes effect (which forms part of the cash equivalent) is reduced by 40%.

(3)   A member of a COSR scheme or an APP scheme will be treated
       as entitled to a full GMP for the purpose of calculating
       entitlement to relevant social security benefits (eg the State
       additional pension). The reason for this is, quite simply, that
       the State is not prepared to fund, indirectly, the pension
       sharing arrangement which the parties have made or which has
       been imposed on them. A member of a contracted-out scheme
       will have entered the scheme on the assumption that he would
       not suffer by paying reduced National Insurance contributions
       because he would be compensated by at least as much from his
       scheme; after pension sharing, he will find that he has lost a
       proportion of his GMP and may be financially disadvantaged
       on retirement. This provision ensures that the State does not
       become liable to make up the resultant shortfall in the GMP or
       protected rights paid by the scheme directly caused by pension
       sharing, and when the transferor's entitlement to additional
       pension is calculated it will be assumed that he is entitled to the
       full GMP to which he would have been entitled if the pension
       sharing had never taken place.

4. Rebuilding pension rights

3.14 A person who has transferred part of his pension to his spouse
has, by definition, suffered a reduction in the value of his pension
fund. He may wish to 'rebuild' the fund, to bring it back, as far as
possible, to its previous value to provide for his retirement. This will
not be as simple as it might seem, due to the limitations on pension
contributions imposed by the Inland Revenue. Pension contributions
to occupational schemes fail to attract tax relief if they are more than
15% of annual salary or result in a pension exceeding two-thirds of
final salary. It seems that the basic principle is to be that, in making
these calculations, the pension debit (the amount transferred) is to
be ignored so that it will be assumed that the debit has never taken
place. This means that the extra contributions which the transferor
could make to rebuild his pension could be severely limited. The

government intends to make a concession[1] which will apply to members of occupational schemes on moderate incomes, namely up to £22,650 per annum. (Note, however, that £22,650 is not a 'band'; someone earning, say, £23,000 would not benefit.) The effect of that easement will be that a person on moderate income will be free to rebuild his or her pension towards the maximum permitted, but within the 15% annual limit on employee contributions that will continue to apply. A higher limit applies to personal pensions, which are not affected by this 'easement'. Here, the limit is 40% of annual earnings which, in the government's view, should enable most people to rebuild their pensions without any easement. It should be noted that a transferee of a pension credit is not affected by the value of the credit and may make further contributions up to the maximum permitted without reference to the value of the credit.

THE EFFECT OF PENSION SHARING ON THE TRANSFEREE

3.15 Having considered the position of the transferor, the position of the transferee after pension sharing must be considered. There is an important distinction to be made between the position of a transferee of part of:

(a) an occupational scheme or personal pension scheme (funded scheme);
(b) an unfunded public service scheme;
(c) an unfunded occupational scheme;
(d) various miscellaneous schemes;
(e) the State pension scheme (as to which, see Chapter 4).

In each case, however, the question to be addressed is what the transferee may do with the share transferred to her and what are her rights under the transferred scheme. The time for implementation of transfer is dealt with separately at **3.28**.

---

1   See Official Report (HC) Standing Committee D, 18 March 1999, col 313 per Mr Stephen Timms MP.

1. Mode of discharge of pension credits (other than State scheme pensions)

3.16 The basic position relating to the rights of the transferee is dealt with in Sch 5 to WRPA 1999, which bears the heading 'Pension credits: mode of discharge'. The Schedule consists of the obligations of the persons responsible for the pension arrangement, ie the fund manager or trustees, and sets out the ways in which such persons may discharge their obligations. Liability in respect of a pension credit may not be discharged otherwise than in accordance with Sch 5.[1] The nature of the obligations depend on the kind of pension scheme in question.

Funded schemes

3.17 The intention behind the provisions in WRPA 1999 is that, where the scheme is a funded occupational scheme or a personal pension scheme, the person responsible for the scheme should first offer to discharge its liability to the transferee for the pension credit by making a transfer payment to a suitable scheme or arrangement of the transferee's choice. This can include conferring rights on the transferee within the scheme (an internal transfer). The transferee will be invited to make a choice as to the destination of the pension credit, and if no choice is made within a specified period the person responsible will decide.

Clearly, before this election is made, a solicitor representing a client in this position will have to ensure that the client obtains proper financial advice not only as to the destination of the credit but also as to whether to take an external transfer. It may be that s 32 buyout policies will (following the Finance Bill 1999) be suitable receiving vehicles. It seems also that the new stakeholder pensions would be suitable because of low charging structures for single lump sum investments. However, it must be emphasised again that expert independent advice will be essential.

---

1   WRPA 1999, s 35.

3.18 Accordingly, para 1 (2) of Sch 5 provides that the trustees or managers of the scheme from which a pension credit derives may discharge their liability in respect of the credit by conferring appropriate rights under that scheme on the person entitled to the credit:

(a)   with his consent; or
(b)   in accordance with regulations made by the Secretary of State.

In other words, the internal transfer may be effected only if the transferee agrees or if regulations so provide. The government intends that the regulations will so provide if the transferee does not provide details of an alternative scheme, and, no doubt, a time-limit will be imposed. 'Appropriate rights' are defined as rights which are conferred with effect from and including the day on which the order or provision under which the credit arises takes effect, and whose value, when calculated in accordance with regulations, equals the amount of the credit.[1]

3.19 It is then provided[2] that the trustees or managers may discharge their liability by paying the amount of the pension credit to 'the person responsible for a qualifying arrangement with a view to acquiring rights under that arrangement for the person entitled to the credit', ie to another pension scheme, providing certain conditions are met. These are:

(a) 'the qualifying arrangement is not disqualified as a destination for the credit'
The arrangements which would or might be disqualified are set out in para 7 of Sch 5. Where the credit derives from a tax approved scheme, the destination must also be tax approved. It is intended to make regulations to provide that only contracted-out occupational schemes, appropriate personal pension schemes and appropriate policies of insurance or annuity contracts will be permitted as destinations for rights derived from contracted-out employment. Regulations will also be used to govern the method by which the

---

1   WRPA 1999, Sch 5, para 5.
2   WRPA 1999, Sch 5, para 1 (3).

scheme actuary calculates the benefits in respect of a pension credit, and to determine the terms of an annuity contract or insurance policy which would make it a suitable destination.

(b) 'the person responsible for that arrangement is able and willing to accept payment in respect of the credit'
This is self-explanatory.

(c) 'payment is made with the consent of the person entitled to the credit or in accordance with regulations made by the Secretary of State'
Where the person entitled to the credit does not consent, transfer may be made only in accordance with regulations. It is thought that these regulations will provide that such a transfer may be made when the person entitled does not provide details of an alternative scheme but the scheme does not want to give that person rights within the scheme. It is also provided that no account will be taken of the consent of the person entitled to credit unless:

(a)   it is given after receipt of notice in writing of an offer to make a payment to another scheme as an external transfer; or
(b)   it is not withdrawn within 7 days of receipt.[1]

What this seems to mean is that the trustees or managers must offer to make an external transfer (presumably to a destination of the transferee's choice), and any consent given may not be acted on for 7 days after receipt.

Unfunded public service pension schemes
3.20   Paragraph 2 of Sch 5 to WRPA 1999 relates to occupational pension schemes which are not funded and which are public service pension schemes. With one exception, the trustees or managers may provide benefits under the scheme only by way of internal transfer;[2] external transfer is not permitted. The exception occurs when the scheme is closed to new members, in which case the transferee may be offered membership of an alternative public service scheme which has been specified by regulations.[3]

---

1   WRPA 1999, Sch 5, para 1(4).
2   WRPA 1999, Sch 5, para 2(2).
3   WRPA 1999, Sch 5, para 2(3) and (4).

3.21 When the trustees or managers have to specify another scheme, they must secure that appropriate rights are conferred on the person entitled to the credit by the trustees or managers of the alternative scheme, and must require them to take such steps as may be required.[1]

Other unfunded occupational pension schemes

3.22 Paragraph 3 of Sch 5 applies when the pension credit is derived from an occupational pension scheme which is not funded and which is not a public service pension scheme. Here, the trustees or managers have a choice, but the choice of the transferee is limited. The trustees or managers:

> '... may discharge their liability in respect of the credit by conferring appropriate rights under that scheme [ie the transferor's scheme] on the person entitled to the credit.'[2]

This would be an internal transfer. They have, therefore, the absolute right to do this and the transferee has no choice. However, they may transfer the credit externally, subject to certain conditions, namely:

(a)   the proposed destination is not disqualified; this has been considered at **3.19**;

(b)   the person responsible for the arrangement proposed as the destination is able and willing to accept payment in respect of the credit;

(c)   payment is made with the consent of the person entitled to the credit or in accordance with regulations.[3]

If the person entitled to credit does not consent, therefore, the transfer may be made only by the authority of regulations. It is intended that the regulations will identify the circumstances in which a transfer without consent would be permissible.

Other pension arrangements

3.23 Paragraph 4 of Sch 5 is limited to pension credits which derive from:

---

1   WRPA 1999, Sch 5, para 2(4).
2   WRPA 1999, Sch 5, para 3(2).
3   WRPA 1999, Sch 5, para 3(3).

(a)   a retirement annuity contract;
(b)   an annuity or insurance policy purchased or transferred for the purpose of giving effect to rights under an occupational pension scheme or a personal pension scheme; or
(c)   an annuity purchased or entered into for the purpose of discharging liability in respect of a pension credit.[1]

3.24 The person responsible for the scheme may discharge his obligations by an external transfer in exactly the same way as a trustee or manager of a funded occupational scheme or a personal pension scheme; this was considered at **3.17–3.19**. The pension arrangement may discharge its obligations by entering into a policy of insurance or an annuity contract with the transferee, provided the transferee consents and the arrangement is not disqualified as a destination.[2] However, it is also provided that the pension arrangement may discharge its obligation by assuming an obligation to provide an annuity even if the transferee does not consent, if this is permitted by regulations.[3] It is intended to use this regulation-making power to deal with the situation where the pension credit is derived from an annuity in payment to the member (ie the transferor).

2. Adjustments to amount of pension credit

3.25 Paragraph 8 of Sch 5 provides for the amount of a pension credit which derives from an occupational pension scheme and which is to be the subject of an external transfer to be reduced when the scheme which is subject to the minimum funding requirement under s 56 of PA 1995 is underfunded on the valuation day. For the purposes of this provision, the valuation day is the day by reference to which the cash equivalent on which the pension credit depends falls to be calculated.[4] It is intended that regulations will prescribe that a scheme is underfunded on the valuation day if the latest actuarial valuation obtained in accordance with s 57 of PA 1995 shows the scheme as having insufficient funds to meet fully its liabilities.

---

1   WRPA 1999, Sch 5, para 4(1).
2   WRPA 1999, Sch 5, para 4(2).
3   WRPA 1999, Sch 5, para 4(3) and (4).
4   WRPA 1999, Sch 5, para 8(3).

Regulations will also prescribe the method for calculation of the reduced credit, which, it seems, will be binding on the transferee only if she has refused an offer from the scheme to provide a pension benefit without reduction in that scheme.

3.26 It is also provided that when a person's shareable rights have become subject to a pension debit, and the person responsible for the pension arrangement makes a payment (presumably to the scheme member) without knowing of that debit, the amount of the credit shall be of such lesser amount as may be determined by regulations.[1] It is intended in this way to protect a scheme against loss arising out of a bona fide payment made in ignorance because of a late notification of a debit.

3.27 Paragraph 10 of Sch 5 provides for increase of the amount of a pension credit where payment is made after the end of the implementation period (as to which, see **3.28** et seq). This is intended to compensate the transferee for delay on the part of the scheme. This will be governed by regulations, but it seems that the method of compensation will be the award of interest.

3. Time for implementation

3.28 Pension sharing can be effected only by the person responsible for the administration of the fund which is the subject of the order or agreement and, if the intentions of the legislation are to be fulfilled, it is necessary to provide for the time within which that person fulfils his obligations. So far in this chapter, we have considered how pension sharing is to be implemented, and the options available to the trustees or managers. This section is concerned only with the time-limits.

3.29 It is provided that a person subject to liability in respect of a pension credit (such as a trustee or manager of a pension fund) must discharge his liability before the end of the implementation period. The implementation period for a pension credit is defined as:

---

1   WRPA 1999, Sch 5, para 9.

'... the period of 4 months beginning with the later of –

(a)   the day on which the relevant order or provision takes effect, and
(b)   the first day on which the person responsible for the pension arrangement to which the relevant order or provision relates is in receipt of –
  (i)   the relevant matrimonial documents, and
  (ii)   such information relating to the transferor and transferee as the Secretary of State may prescribe by regulations.'[1]

3.30   The position is, therefore, that, once the relevant documents have been served on the person responsible, he has 4 months from that date to make arrangements for the credit, unless the date on which the order or agreement takes effect is more than 4 months in the future, in which case it is the latter date. The relevant documents to be served on the responsible person are:

(a)   the order or provision (ie agreement) which gives rise to the pension sharing; and
(b)   the order or decree responsible for the divorce or annulment between the parties.[2]

In addition, it will be necessary to send such documents or information as may be prescribed by regulations. It is thought that this may include such information as the couple's full names, addresses, ages and national insurance numbers.

3.31   Section 34 of WRPA 1999 also contains power to make regulations as to various further matters. These may include the right of the responsible person to delay payment of the credit until any charges made by him have been paid; an obligation on the responsible person to inform both transferor and transferee of the date on which the implementation period begins; and for the

---

1   WRPA 1999, s 34(1).
2   WRPA 1999, s 34(2).

implementation period to be suspended when an application is being made for leave to appeal out of time.[1]

3.32 When trustees or managers of an occupational pension scheme have not done what is required to discharge their liability before the end of the implementation period, they may have to inform the regulatory authority of that fact within a prescribed period. This may render them liable to penalties under s 10 of PA 1995.[2]

3.33 In the event of the death of the person entitled to the pension credit before liability for the credit has been discharged, Sch 5 (which sets out the methods by which liability may be discharged) ceases to have effect, and the liability of the person responsible will be discharged in accordance with regulations.[3] It is thought that these regulations will provide that the deceased former spouse shall be treated as if she had become a member of the scheme in question. This might have the result, for example, that, where the pension credit had been derived from the member's personal pension scheme, the personal pension provider would be required to pay the amount of the pension credit to the deceased former spouse's estate.

4. Provisions governing the treatment of pension credit rights

3.34 Special provisions have been made to ensure, so far as possible, that the rights of a former spouse who becomes a member of a scheme by virtue of pension sharing are protected. These may be categorised as safeguarded rights and other rights, and are to be effected by amendments made to PSA 1993.

Safeguarded rights
3.35 Section 36 of WRPA 1999 inserts a new Part IIIA into PSA 1993. Part IIIA makes special provision for the pension credit rights of a

---

1   WRPA 1999, s 34(4).
2   WRPA 1999, s 33.
3   WRPA 1999, s 35.

former spouse deriving from membership of a contracted-out occupational pension scheme or an appropriate personal pension scheme. These rights are called 'safeguarded rights' to distinguish them from the contracted-out rights built up by members of such schemes, but the intention is that the requirements for safeguarded rights should broadly equate to those for contracted-out rights. In particular, it is intended to ensure that safeguarded rights are securely protected and used for their intended purpose, namely to provide an income in retirement.

3.36 The provisions are contained in the new ss 68A–68C of PSA 1993, and since they are of only marginal interest to family lawyers, will not be summarised further here.

Other rights
3.37 Section 37 of WRPA 1999 also makes amendments to PSA 1993 to regulate the treatment of pension credit rights in various respects. They fall into two broad categories, and may be summarised as follows.

(1) The first main category of rights are those designed to ensure that rights in an occupational pension scheme which are derived from a pension credit are treated in a way broadly similar to the way in which the rights of deferred members are required to be treated under Chapter 1 of Part IV of PSA 1993. This part of the new provisions apply to all types of occupational pension schemes.

The new ss 101A–101E of PSA 1993 provide for such matters as the availability of early payment of pension, payment in lump sum form in certain circumstances, transfer of pension credit benefit from one scheme or arrangement to another, the protection of early leavers, and the discharge of the provider's responsibility by purchase of an annuity or policy of insurance.

(2) The second main category relate to the right of members of funded occupational and personal pension schemes whose rights derive from a pension credit to transfer to another pension scheme or arrangement. This is achieved by inserting new ss 101F–101Q into PSA 1993. The provisions are complicated and need not be set out here in detail, but essentially

enable a former spouse with pension credit rights the right to transfer to another scheme in the same way as an early leaver. However, this does not extend to unfunded schemes.

The provisions deal with such matters as the form of notice, the valuation of cash equivalents, limitations on the right to transfer, liability of trustees or managers for breach, and the position when the scheme is underfunded. It should also be noted that s 38 of WRPA 1999 deals with the priority of pension credit rights on the winding up of an occupational pension scheme.

5. Indexation of public service and other schemes

3.38 One of the advantages of certain pension schemes is the fact that they are index-linked, and that the payments from them increase regularly in accordance with some yardstick such as the cost of living index. A former spouse acquiring rights in such a scheme by pension sharing will naturally wish to share in that benefit.

The indexation of public service schemes such as those for civil servants, teachers, NHS staff and so on derives from the Pensions (Increase) Act 1971, and s 39 of WRPA 1999 therefore amends that Act to confer on persons acquiring rights by pension credit similar rights to those enjoyed by the scheme member.

3.39 Indexation is also available in schemes other than public service schemes, and s 40 therefore confers on the Secretary of State a set of rule-making powers to govern such schemes. In outline, they are intended to enable the Secretary of State to protect occupational schemes and personal pension schemes from inflation.

CHARGES BY PENSION ARRANGEMENTS

3.40 One of the features of the pension sharing provisions is that pension schemes and arrangements are to be entitled to charge fees for dealing with pension debits and credits, with the intention, no doubt, of avoiding cost to other members of the scheme. It is not intended that charges should be compulsory, but that schemes should be able to charge if they so desire; in such cases, the charges will be regulated. These matters are governed by s 41 of WRPA 1999. The Act gives no indication of what the amount of such charges is likely to be but, in cases where the parties have limited means, it may be wise to make specific provision as to which party is to be responsible for the charges; this is considered further below.

3.41 Section 41 of WRPA 1999 is, in fact, a regulation-making provision, and the detail of all these provisions is to be contained in regulations. Subsection (2) sets out the matters with which such regulations may deal, as follows:

(a)   provision for the start of the implementation period to be postponed. The intention is that it may be permissible to postpone dealing with a pension credit until charges have been paid;

(b)   provision for reimbursement between the parties of the charges;

(c)   provision for recovery of charges by deduction from a pension credit;

(d)   provision for additional charges, for example when charges are not paid on time.

3.42 Section 41(3) makes further provision to govern apportionment of charges between parties. The provisions may be summarised as follows:

(a)   when the relevant court order or agreement which created the pension debit and credit made specific provision for the apportionment of charges, the parties will bear the charges as provided. This is clearly the best solution, to avoid misunderstanding;

(b)   where the order or agreement does not include such a provision, the charge will fall on the transferor.

JUDICIAL PENSIONS

3.43 Members of the judiciary in the UK are entitled to a pension by virtue of either the Judicial Pensions Act 1991, the Judicial Pensions and Retirement Act 1993 or the Sheriff's Pensions (Scotland) Act 1961. Section 43 of WRPA 1999 confers on the appropriate minister (in England and Wales, the Lord Chancellor) the power to make regulations in effect to bring about pensions sharing, so that the former spouse of a member of the judiciary will be able to obtain a credit in the pension scheme with the same benefits (eg as to index linking) as the scheme member.

Chapter 4

PENSION SHARING AND STATE SCHEME RIGHTS

INTRODUCTION

4.1 Chapters 2 and 3 have been concerned with the nature of pension sharing and the effect of pension sharing in relation to occupational and personal pension schemes of various kinds. However, in addition to these provisions, pension sharing is available in relation to the State scheme pension, as defined below. Since these are distinct provisions, it seems convenient to deal with them in a separate chapter. The matters to be considered in this chapter are the meaning of pension sharing in this context, and the effect of any order or agreement.

WHAT STATE SCHEME PENSIONS MAY BE SHARED?

4.2 Not all State scheme pensions are subject to pension sharing; most significantly, the basic retirement pension is not included.

It is provided that:

'... a person's shareable state scheme rights are –

(a) his entitlement, or prospective entitlement, to a Category A retirement pension by virtue of section 44(3)(b) of the Social Security Contributions and Benefits Act (earnings-related additional pension), and

(b) his entitlement, or prospective entitlement, to a pension under section 55A of that Act (shared additional pension).'[1]

This definition requires little comment. Essentially, this form of pension sharing is limited to SERPS rights either earned by a person

---
1   WRPA 1999, s 47(2).

in his own right by paying standard rate Class 1 National Insurance contributions or derived from a pension share in respect of previous matrimonial proceedings; the pension derived from a State scheme pension credit is to be called a 'shared additional pension'. The prospective amount of any person's entitlement to either of these benefits is always available on the enquiry of that person, and, no doubt, the courts will regularly be asked to require this information to be supplied.

ACTIVATION OF PENSION SHARING

4.3   The circumstances in which pension sharing is activated are set out in s 48(1) of WRPA 1999. These circumstances or events are identical with those for non State schemes as set out in s 28(1) (as to which, see **2.12** et seq) and need not be repeated here.

THE EFFECT OF SHARING OF STATE SCHEME RIGHTS

4.4   The creation of State scheme pension debits and credits is governed by s 49(1) of WRPA 1999. It is provided that this section applies on the taking effect of any of the events set out in s 45, and that then:

> '(a) the transferor becomes subject, for the purposes of Part II of the Contributions and Benefits Act (contributory benefits), to a debit of the appropriate amount, and
> (b) the transferee becomes entitled, for those purposes, to a credit of that amount.'[1]

The order or provision must specify a percentage to be transferred, and the appropriate amount is defined as 'the specified percentage of the cash equivalent on the transfer day of the transferor's shareable

---

1   WRPA 1999, s 49(1).

State scheme rights immediately before that day.'[1] The transfer day is the day on which the order or provision takes effect.[2]

4.5 Essentially, therefore, the transferor's additional pension is reduced by the amount of the debit, and the transferee becomes entitled to an additional pension in his own right based on the pension credit. The effect is set out in detail in Sch 6 to WRPA 1999, which inserts a new s 45B into the Social Security Contributions and Benefits Act 1992.

It is intended that regulations will govern the calculation of the cash equivalent. It is provided that, in determining prospective entitlement to a Category A retirement pension for the purposes of this section, only tax years before the year in which the transfer day falls will be taken into account.[3]

4.6 The amount of the reduction of the additional pension caused by pension sharing depends on the age of the transferor on the transfer day. If a person becomes subject to the debit in or after 'the final relevant year', that is to say the tax year immediately before he reaches pensionable age,[4] the additional pension will be reduced by 'the appropriate weekly amount';[5] this is a weekly amount which is of an actuarially equivalent value to the State scheme debit.[6] Assuming, therefore, that pensionable age is 65, this provision would apply when the debit took effect not earlier than the tax year in which the transferor attained the age of 65. Where the debit is made 'before the relevant year', ie before the tax year immediately before the transferor attains pensionable age, the additional pension will be reduced by 'the appropriate weekly amount multiplied by the

---

1   WRPA 1999, s 49(2).
2   WRPA 1999, s 49(6).
3   WRPA 1999, s 49(5).
4   Social Security Contributions and Benefits Act 1992, s 45B(8) (as amended by WRPA 1999, Sch 6).
5   Social Security Contributions and Benefits Act 1992, s 45B (as amended by WRPA 1999, Sch 6, para 2).
6   This is the effect of Social Security Contributions and Benefits Act 1992, s 45B(4).

relevant revaluation percentage'.[1] This means the weekly amount referred to above, multiplied by the earnings factor percentage for the relevant tax year specified in the latest annual Revaluation of Earnings Factor Order.

4.7   The new ss 55A–55C of the Social Security Contributions and Benefits Act 1992 inserted by Sch 6 to WRPA 1999 deal with the meaning of 'shared additional pension'. This term is significant in two respects.

(1)   Pension sharing may occur in relation to a shared additional pension, so it is necessary for an applicant to know exactly what it is.

(2)   The effect on a shared additional pension of pension sharing (one might say 'further pension sharing') must be considered.

4.8   A person becomes entitled to a shared additional pension if he is:

(a)   over pensionable age; and

(b)   entitled to a State scheme pension credit.[2]

The entitlement cannot, therefore, arise until the person concerned (the transferee under the pension sharing) attains pensionable age. For the avoidance of doubt, it should be noted that the transferor need not yet have attained pensionable age, and could be younger than the transferee; the original pension sharing arrangement would have been calculated on the basis of his accrued entitlement. The requirement for a State scheme pension credit is obvious; there must have been a pension sharing arrangement.

4.9   The process for determining the weekly amount of the shared additional pension to which the transferee is entitled is exactly the same as that set out at **4.6**.

---

1   Social Security Contributions and Benefits Act 1992, s 45B(3).
2   Social Security Contributions and Benefits Act 1992, s 55A(1).

4.10   It is provided that a person's entitlement to a shared additional pension will continue throughout his life.[1] Once the pension is in payment, it will be increased by the same percentage as other pensions on an annual basis. Where a person's entitlement to a shared additional pension is deferred, the rate of his shared additional pension is increased by a formula contained in the new s 55C(2).

PENSION SHARING IN RESPECT OF A SHARED ADDITIONAL PENSION

4.11   Having considered the significance of the shared additional pension in the most common case, namely a person (normally a wife) acquiring by means of pension transfer a share in her former spouse's SERPS entitlement, it is now necessary to consider the further circumstances in which this may be relevant. These arise out of the fact that a shared additional pension acquired in this conventional way may itself be the subject of pension sharing in favour of a subsequent former spouse.

4.12   It is provided that the weekly amount of a shared additional pension will be reduced in any case where:

(a)   the pensioner has become subject to a State scheme pension debit; and

(b)   the debit is to any extent referable to the pension.[2]

This assumes that the pensioner (the transferor) is entitled to a shared additional pension. It is contemplated that the pension debit may have occurred before the pensioner attains pensionable age since the same formula as that set out at **4.6** is used to calculate the weekly rate of the reductions.[3]

---

1   Social Security Contributions and Benefits Act 1992, s 55A(2).
2   Social Security Contributions and Benefits Act 1992, s 55B(1).
3   See Social Security Contributions and Benefits Act 1992, s 55B(2) to (4).

Chapter 5

APPEALS AND VARIATION

INTRODUCTION

5.1 All orders for ancillary relief may be set aside on appeal, and some can be varied; the general rule is that a final capital order cannot be varied. Pension sharing orders are no exception to the general rule as to appeals but, because of the nature of pension sharing and the need to protect pension providers, it has been necessary to make some special provisions as to appeal and variation. These will be considered in turn.

APPEALS

5.2 The only type of pension sharing which may be appealed is, of course, an order for pension sharing made under s 21A of MCA 1973. It is unclear what would happen if someone wished to disturb the terms of a pension sharing brought about by an agreement made after the coming into force of Part II of FLA 1996.

5.3 The procedure for any appeal will depend on whether or not the pension sharing order has taken effect. It will be remembered that the court has a duty to stay all pension sharing orders for a prescribed period, and it is provided that no pension sharing order may be made so as to take effect before the end of such period after the making of the order as may be prescribed by rules made by the Lord Chancellor.[1] This is to allow the parties an opportunity to appeal or apply to vary the order. Any appeal within that period will be subject to no restrictions and regulations will provide that the order continues to be stayed until the appeal has been disposed of. The period of the stay will be determined by regulations. The draft

---

1   MCA 1973, s 24C(1).

regulations (reg 11) provide that no pension sharing order or variation of a pension sharing order may take effect earlier than seven days after the end of the period for filing notice of appeal against the order; the period of say will, therefore, depend on the time-limits for appeal from the court in question. It is also provided that the filing of a notice of appeal within the time allowed for doing so prevents the order taking effect before the appeal has been dealt with. It should be remembered that no pension sharing order can take effect in any event until the decree has been made absolute or, after the coming into force of Part II of FLA 1996, a divorce order or decree absolute of nullity has been granted.

5.4   The position is different where the order has already taken effect, that is to say, the person responsible for the pension arrangement may have given effect to the order by creating a pension credit in favour of the transferee. Here the appeal will be out of time, and the court would have to grant leave on the usual principles (eg *Barder v Caluori*[1]). Where an appeal is begun on or after the day on which the order takes effect, the provisions of the new MCA 1973, s 40A(2) and (3) will apply. It is first provided that if the pension sharing order relates to a person's rights under a pension arrangement, the appeal court may not set aside or vary the order if the person responsible for the pension arrangement has acted to his detriment in reliance on the taking effect of the order.[2] It is clearly envisaged that the person responsible will have to be served with notice of any appeal and will be entitled to make representations on the hearing of the appeal. The court would have to make a decision on the issue. There are then similar provisions to protect the Secretary of State where the pension sharing order relates to a person's shareable State scheme rights.[3] In determining whether a person has acted to his detriment in reliance on the taking effect of the order, the appeal court may disregard any detriment which in its opinion is insignificant.[4]

---

1   [1988] AC 20, [1987] 2 FLR 480, HL.
2   MCA 1973, s 40A(2).
3   MCA 1973, s 40A(3).
4   MCA 1973, s 40A(4).

5.5 'Appeal court' is not defined, but it would seem that it must include a judge hearing an appeal from an order made by a district judge.

5.6 The section goes on to provide additional powers for the appeal court in these circumstances. When s 40A(2) or (3) apply (that is to say, the court may not set aside or vary the order because of some perceived detriment), the appeal court may make such further orders (including one or more pension sharing orders) as it thinks fit for the purpose of putting the parties into the position it considers appropriate.[1] This should ensure that the appeal court deals finally with the matter, rather than sending it back for reconsideration or merely deleting the offending provision. It might also mean that the appeal court could, in suitable circumstances, make orders to compensate a party where it would have allowed an appeal but for the fact that the person responsible for the pension arrangement had acted to his detriment.

Any pension sharing order made by an appeal court would be subject to the same duty to stay pending a prescribed period except where the order of the appeal court was not itself subject to appeal;[2] this would apply only to the House of Lords.

VARIATION

5.7 There is no provision for variation of a pension sharing order made after a decree has been made absolute[3] or, after the coming into force of Part II of FLA 1996, a divorce order has been made. Once the decree is made absolute or, as the case may be, a divorce order is made, therefore, the only remedy available to someone aggrieved by an order would be to appeal. However, if the order was made at a time when the decree had not been made absolute (or the divorce order had not yet been made), the order could not yet have

---

1   MCA 1973, s 40A(5).
2   MCA 1973, s 40A(6).
3   MCA 1973, s 31(2)(g).

taken effect, and the position is different. Section 31(2) of MCA 1973, which contains the classes of orders capable of variation, now includes at para (g):

> 'a pension sharing order under section 24B ... which is made at a time before the decree has been made absolute.'

5.8   Therefore, such an order may be varied. Any application for variation would be considered in the light of s 31 of MCA 1973 and would be to that extent a normal variation application; no doubt it would be necessary to show some change in circumstances before a variation order could be made.

5.9   There are further restrictions on the making of such an application to vary. It is provided that the powers conferred by s 31 (ie the power to vary) may be exercised:

> '(i)   only on an application made before the [pension sharing order] has or, but for paragraph (b) below, would have taken effect; and
>
> (ii) only if, at the time when the application is made, the decree has not been made absolute.'[1]

Paragraph (b) provides that an application made in accordance with the above provisions prevents the pension sharing order from taking effect before the application has been dealt with.[2]

5.10   The result of all this seems to be as follows.

(1)   An application to vary a pension sharing order can only be made if, at the time the application is made, the decree has not been made absolute. By definition, in such circumstances, the order would have been made before decree absolute.

(2)   An application can be made only if the pension sharing order has not yet taken effect, or would have taken effect if the application to vary had not been made (the application to vary in itself prevents the order taking effect).

---

1   MCA 1973, s 31(4A).
2   MCA 1973, s 31(4A)(b).

At first sight, it might seem that the second provision is unnecessary since, in any event, a pension sharing order cannot take effect before decree absolute. It would appear, therefore, that this provision is required to cater for the possibility that, an application to vary having been made before decree absolute, the decree is then made absolute (since it appears that the application in itself will not prevent the decree being made absolute) and the time stated in the order for it to take effect has passed.

5.11 It is also provided that no variation of a pension sharing order may be made so as to take effect before decree absolute.[1]

---

1   MCA 1973, s 31(4B).

Chapter 6

OTHER CHANGES EFFECTED BY THE ACT

INTRODUCTION

6.1   As has been seen in earlier chapters, the principal effect of Parts III and IV of WRPA 1999 is the introduction into the law and practice of ancillary relief of pension sharing. However, the Act also takes the opportunity to amend the existing law relating to pensions in certain limited respects. The intention of this part of the legislation is to make the law relating to, for example, earmarking, consistent with the new law as to pension sharing. These changes will be examined in turn.

AMENDMENTS TO MFPA 1984

6.2   Part III of MFPA 1984 provides for orders for ancillary relief to be made by the courts of England and Wales after a marriage has been dissolved or annulled or parties have been legally separated by means of judicial or other proceedings in an overseas country and that divorce etc is entitled to be recognised as valid here.[1] The applicant must establish that the court has jurisdiction[2] and the first step is an application for leave. Once leave has been granted, the court has broadly the same powers as it has when dealing with any ancillary relief application.[3] The amendments to MFPA 1984 effected by WRPA 1999 are designed to bring the relief which can be granted into line with that now available under MCA 1973.

---

1   MFPA 1984, s 12(1).
2   Pursuant to MFPA 1984, s 12(2).
3   See MFPA 1984, ss 14 and 17 to 26.

6.3 Section 18 of MFPA 1984 sets out the matters to which the court is to have regard when making an order pursuant to the Act. A new subsection 3A is introduced providing that the matters to which the court must have regard:

> '(a) so far as relating to paragraph (a) of section 25 of the 1973 Act, include any benefits under a pension arrangement which a party to the marriage has or is likely to have (whether or not in the foreseeable future), and
>
> (b) so far as relating to paragraph (h) of that provision, include any benefits under a pension arrangement which, by reason of the dissolution or annulment of the marriage, a party to the marriage will lose the chance of acquiring.'[1]

'Pension arrangement' has the same meaning as in MCA 1973, s 25D(3).[2]

6.4 The 1984 Act already provides that, except where jurisdiction is founded only on the situation in England and Wales of a dwellinghouse which was a matrimonial home of the parties, the court has power to make any financial provision order or property adjustment order,[3] and various sections of MCA 1973 which provide for the different types of order are applied.[4] Since MCA 1973 itself is amended by WRPA 1999 to include orders for pension sharing, it follows that pension sharing will be one of the orders which may be made under MFPA 1984.

However, MFPA 1984 is specifically amended so that s 21 includes s 25B(3)–(7B) of MCA 1973, which are the provisions for earmarking and requiring the exercise of a right of commutation, and s 25C of MCA 1973 which is the extension of lump sum powers in relation to death benefits under a pension arrangement.[5] These provisions do not apply when the only basis for jurisdiction was the situation in

---

1   WRPA 1999, s 22(2).
2   WRPA 1999, s 22(3).
3   MFPA 1984, s 17.
4   MFPA 1984, s 21.
5   WRPA 1999, s 22(4).

England and Wales of a dwellinghouse which was the matrimonial home of the parties.[1]

6.5 The combined effect of these provisions is, therefore, that the powers available under MFPA 1984 are broadly the same as those contained in MCA 1973.

AMENDMENTS TO MCA 1973, SECTIONS 25B TO 25D

6.6 Schedule 4 to WRPA 1999 is headed 'amendments of sections 25B to 25D MCA', and contains amendments some of which are minor and some more important. Many of the amendments do no more than reflect the new terminology, so that 'arrangement' replaces 'scheme' and 'person responsible for' an arrangement replaces 'trustee or manager'. There are also provisions which ensure that terms such as 'pension arrangement' bear the same meaning as elsewhere in the Act. These are, essentially, tidying up amendments and need not be recited in detail. Readers are referred for the detail to the amended MCA 1973 set out in the Appendix to this book.

6.7 However, two of the amendments are of some substance. It is provided by a new s 25B(7A) that the power to make an earmarking order under s 25B(4) and the power to require commutation under s 25B(7) may not be exercised in relation to a pension arrangement which:

(a) is the subject of a pension sharing order in relation to the marriage; or
(b) has been the subject of pension sharing between the parties to the marriage.[2]

The effect of this is, first, that in relation to any particular pension arrangement a choice has to be made as to whether to invoke

---

1   WRPA 1999, s 22(5).
2   WRPA 1999, Sch 4, para 1(9).

earmarking (or the right to require commutation) or pension sharing. It is not possible to make orders of both types affecting the same arrangement. This topic will be discussed in more detail in Chapter 7. Secondly, the effect of the new s 25B(7) is that the court may order a person with pension rights not to commute.

AMENDMENTS TO THE INSOLVENCY ACT 1986

6.8   Schedule 12 to WRPA 1999 makes certain amendments to the Insolvency Act 1986 which should be noted by family lawyers, although it is fair to say that they do not change any fundamental principles; rather, they ensure that pension sharing is no exception to the established law relating to other financial provision orders. The circumstances in which these questions may become relevant are where a bankruptcy order is made after a financial provision order (in this case, a pension sharing order) has been made; what effect does the bankruptcy order have on the order and its implementation?

6.9   In the case of a property adjustment order, the trustee in bankruptcy may apply to the court for an order to set aside any transaction 'at an undervalue' made within a specified period before the day of the presentation of the bankruptcy petition.[1] The fact that the transaction has been made pursuant to a court order does not affect the position.[2] The specified period is five years unless it can be shown that the transferor was not insolvent at the date of the transaction and that he did not become insolvent because of it.[3] A lump sum order may be attacked by a trustee in bankruptcy on the ground that it constitutes a preference. Where a bankrupt has given a preference within the time specified by the 1986 Act (normally five years, as in the case of a property adjustment order), the court may make such order as is necessary to restore the position to what it would have been if the preference had not been made.[4]

---

1   Insolvency Act 1986, s 339.
2   MCA 1973, s 39.
3   See Insolvency Act 1986, s 341.
4   Insolvency Act 1986, s 340(1) and (2).

6.10 Another problem arises under the present law in relation to earmarking orders made in relation to benefits payable under a policy or scheme when a bankruptcy order is made against the policy holder or scheme member. The impact of the bankruptcy order will depend on the nature of the pension arrangements and the terms of the scheme. Essentially, the member's rights under the policy are a chose in action and thus 'property' within the meaning of s 46 of the Insolvency Act 1986, with the result that they vest immediately in the trustee in bankruptcy unless the scheme contains a forfeiture clause which provides that, on bankruptcy, the member's rights are forfeited and vest in the trustees on a discretionary trust. Not every forfeiture clause achieves this result, and the outcome of any case will depend on the circumstances of the case and the wording of the documents.[1]

6.11 When s 91(3) of the Pensions Act 1995 comes into force, a member of an occupational scheme will be in a better position than the holder of a personal pension policy or retirement annuity contract in the event of the making of a bankruptcy order against him. Under s 91(1), a member of an occupational scheme who is entitled, or has an accrued right, to a pension under that scheme is prohibited from assigning, commuting or surrendering that entitlement or right. Under s 91(3), where a bankruptcy order is made against any person, any entitlement or right which cannot be assigned is excluded from his estate and will not vest in the trustee.

6.12 It is against this background that the amendments to the Insolvency Act 1986 contained in para 69 of Sch 12 to WRPA 1999 are made. It is unnecessary to set out all the detail here (interested readers will find it in the Appendix to this book) and the principal features will be summarised. The marginal note to the new provisions reads 'recovery of excessive contributions in pension sharing cases' which, in effect, summarises the purpose of the provisions. A pension sharing transaction (defined[2] as an order or provision falling within

---

1   See eg *Re L (A Bankrupt)* [1997] 2 FLR 660, and *Re Trusts of the Scientific Investment Pension Plan* [1998] 2 FLR 761.
2   By the Insolvency Act 1986, s 342D(9).

s 28(1) of WRPA 1999, ie orders and agreements which activate
pension sharing) shall be taken to be capable of being a transaction
entered into at an undervalue only so far as it is a transfer of so much
of the appropriate amount as represents excessive contributions.[1]
Similarly, such a transaction shall be taken to be capable of being a
preference given to the transferee only so far as it is a transfer of so
much of the appropriate amount as represents excessive contributions.[2] 'Appropriate amount' means, in effect, the same as in
WRPA 1999, s 29(2), namely the specified percentage of the CETV
which is to be transferred.[3]

6.13 The question of whether any pension sharing transaction
represents excessive contributions must be decided in accordance
with subss (4)–(8) of s 342D.[4] The essence of these provisions is that
the court must decide whether, and if so, to what extent, the
transferor's rights under the pension arrangement at the time of the
pension sharing appear to have been the fruits of contributions
(defined as 'personal contributions') which the transferor has at any
time made on his own behalf or which have at any time been made on
the transferor's behalf. Where it appears that those rights were to any
extent the fruits of personal contributions the court must then
determine the extent (if any) to which those rights appear to have
been the fruits of personal contributions whose making has unfairly
prejudiced the transferor's creditors; those contributions are called
'unfair contributions'.

6.14 In making its decision as to whether any personal contributions
were unfair contributions, the court is directed in particular to
consider whether any of the personal contributions were made for
the purpose of putting assets beyond the reach of the transferor's
creditors, and also whether the total amount of the personal
contributions represented, at the time of the pension sharing
transaction, was an amount which was excessive in view of the

---

1   Insolvency Act 1986, s 342D(1)(a).
2   Insolvency Act 1986, s 342D(2)(b).
3   Insolvency Act 1986, s 342D(9).
4   Insolvency Act 1986, s 342D(3).

transferor's circumstances at that time. Having made a finding that the contributions, or some part of them, were unfair contributions, the court must then go on to decide whether the extent to which the transferor's rights were unfair contributions is such that the transfer made under the pension sharing arrangement could not have been made out of the transferor's rights were it not for the unfair contributions. Where the transfer could not have been wholly so made without the unfair contributions, then the amount transferred represent excessive contributions to the extent that it could not have been made without them. Where the transfer could have been made without the unfair contributions, there are no excessive contributions.

6.15 If a court finds that there have been excessive contributions, it will then make a finding that the transaction was entered into either at an undervalue or that it was a preference. Sections 342E and 342F then deal with the right of the trustee in bankruptcy to obtain payment from the 'person responsible for the destination arrangement' (ie the trustees or managers of the pension arrangement into which the transferee's pension credit has found its way), and the right of the trustee to demand information from such persons.

Chapter 7

PENSION SHARING IN PRACTICE

INTRODUCTION

7.1   In previous chapters of this book, the author's intention has been to set out the provisions of Parts III and IV of WRPA 1999 and to explain what is likely to be their effect in practice when they come into force, probably some time in 2001. In this chapter, it is intended to consider the wider picture, and to put pension sharing not only in the context of the other provisions relating to pensions contained in MCA 1973, but also in the context of ancillary relief generally. When WRPA 1999 comes into force, the practitioner will have to decide how significant pensions really are in the case under consideration, and also which of the various available forms of relief he should seek to achieve. It is hoped that this chapter may assist in that process.

SOME GENERAL PRINCIPLES OF ANCILLARY RELIEF

7.2   At the risk of being pedantic or simplistic, the point must be made that pensions are merely one aspect of ancillary relief, and are not some discrete form of relief. If there ever were any doubts about this proposition, they must have been put at rest by the decision of Singer J in *T v T (Financial Relief: Pensions)*.[1] In that case, it was argued that the amendments to MCA 1973 brought about by the Pensions Act 1995 manifested an intention by the legislature to require, and not just enable, a non-pension scheme member spouse to be compensated for her actual and potential loss of pension benefits. It was also asserted that this compensatory principle encompassed not only the pension which would be hers by right if as his widow she

---

1   [1998] 1 FLR 1072.

survived him on his death, whether before or after his retirement, but also her 'share' of the benefits she would derive as his wife if she was still his wife once the husband started to draw his benefits.

7.3　Singer J rejected this argument. Such a proposition, if accepted, would have the effect of turning on its head the court's established approach under s 25 of MCA 1973. It would mean that the provision to be made from pensions would be considered uniquely as a matter of right and entitlement. He concluded that there might be cases where the circumstances would justify such prominence being given to pension rights but this was not one of them. He also observed that the statute required the court 'in particular' to 'have regard' to the pension benefits etc, and to consider how the pension consider-ations 'should affect' the terms of the order it intended to make. That formulation in no way precluded the court from giving the answer 'not at all' to that question.

7.4　The basic principle therefore remains. In a recent authoritat-ive decision,[1] Thorpe LJ drew attention to the fact that even prior to the deletion in 1984 of the statutory duty to attempt to put the parties in the financial position in which they would have been had the marriage not broken down, the Court of Appeal[2] had defined the judge's ultimate aim as being to do that which was fair, just and reasonable between the parties, and that had continued to be the judicial interpretation of the objective of s 25. Parliament had not chosen to lay any emphasis on any one of the eight specific factors above any other.[3] Thorpe LJ continued:

> 'Although there is no ranking of the criteria to be found in the statute, there is as it were a magnetism that draws the individual case to attach to one, two, or several factors as having decisive influence on its determination.'[4]

He concluded this part of his judgment as follows:

1　*White v White* [1998] 2 FLR 310.
2　In *Page v Page* [1981] 2 FLR 198, CA at 206.
3　See also *Smith v Smith* [1991] 2 FLR 432, CA per Butler-Sloss LJ.
4　[1998] 2 FLR 310 at 317.

'It has often been said, and cannot be too often repeated, that each case depends on its own unique facts and those facts must determine which of the eight factors is to be given particular prominence in determination.'[1]

7.5 It is against that background that the specific duties of the court in relation to pensions must be considered.

THE COURT'S DUTY WITH REGARD TO PENSIONS

7.6 Section 25 of MCA 1973 provides that the court must 'have regard' to 'all the circumstances' and, in particular, to the factors listed in s 25(2). It is then provided that the matters to which the court is to have regard under s 25(2) include, in the case of paragraph (a) which is that which deals with the income, property and other financial resources of the parties:

'... any benefits under a pension arrangement which a party to the marriage has or is likely to have,'

and, in the case of paragraph (h), which deals with the value to the parties of any benefit which, by reason of the dissolution or annulment of the marriage, a party will lose the chance of acquiring:

'... any benefits under a pension arrangement which ... a party to the marriage will lose the chance of acquiring.'[2]

It is also specifically provided that, in case of paragraph (a), in relation to benefits under a pension arrangement, the section is to be read as if the words 'in the foreseeable future' were omitted.[3] The significance of this is that any pension benefits which either party is likely to acquire at any time, however far distant it may be, fall to be considered by the court.

---

1   [1998] 2 FLR 310 at 318.
2   MCA 1973, s 25B(1)(a).
3   MCA 1973, s 25B(1)(b).

7.7   It should be noted that the existing s 25B(2), which requires the court to consider whether, in the light of any benefits under a pension scheme, a financial provision order should be made, and, if so, how the terms of the order should be affected by such matters, is deleted in its entirety by WRPA 1999, so that duty will no longer exist when WRPA 1999 comes into force (of course, it remains applicable until then). The statutory matters to which the court must have regard are those set out at **7.5** above, subject to the words of guidance at **7.3**.

The court is therefore directed to have regard to the existence or potential existence of pension benefits and the loss or potential loss of such benefits. It must decide how to exercise its powers, including the new powers conferred on it by the amendments to MCA 1973 effected by WRPA 1999, as part of the whole picture, and in an attempt to do that which is 'fair, just and reasonable' between the parties.

THE POWERS OF THE COURT AFTER THE WRPA 1999

7.8   As was outlined in Chapter 1, the ways in which the court will be able to deal with pensions are as follows:

(1)   to treat them as a resource of one of the parties and, if appropriate, to 'offset' them against some other asset, for example by awarding the other party a greater share of the other assets than would otherwise have been the case;

(2)   to use the powers of earmarking under s 25B to require the trustees or managers of the pension scheme or arrangement to pay to the non-scheme member sums of money which would otherwise have been paid to the member, or under s 25C which deals with payments to be made after the scheme member's death. Section 25B is, in effect, a means of enforcing an order for periodical payments or for a lump sum against the pension arrangement. In addition to this power, the power to require the pension arrangement member to commute all or part of his pension entitlement may be invoked;

(3)   to make an order for pension sharing.

7.9   It will always be possible to offset, and to award one party a larger share of assets at the same time as using options 2 or 3 above; this would be regarded as being part of an overall package. However, it is provided that a pension sharing order may not be made in relation to the rights of a person under a pension arrangement if there is in force a requirement imposed by virtue of s 25B or s 25C which relates to benefits or future benefits to which he is entitled under the pension arrangement.[1] This may mean one of two things. First, it might mean that no pension sharing order might be made if someone, presumably a former spouse, has an earmarking order directed to that pension arrangement already. Secondly, it might (also) mean that the court may not make both a pension sharing order and an earmarking order in respect of the same pension arrangement; while this would not be common, one can foresee circumstancess in which a wife who was otherwise content to have a clean break and a share of a pension would also like to earmark death-in-service benefits to protect her children in the event of the father's death and consequent inability to make the child support payments. It should be noted that neither earmarking nor pension sharing is available for the protection of children's orders. It seems that the official view is that the second interpretation is correct. If this is so, the legislation may well result in injustice. Some of the considerations which may arise will now be examined.

WHAT IS THE COURT TRYING TO DO?

7.10   Before considering the question of how the court's armoury of powers should be deployed, the more fundamental question of what the court is trying to do in any particular case will have to be considered. It has been seen at **7.3** above that pensions must be regarded as being part of the overall picture. The value of any benefits or potential benefits under the pension arrangement must first be ascertained; this has to be by way of the CETV, but evidence

---

1   MCA 1973, s 24B(5).

may be admissible to show that the CETV figure understates the true value. Once the value is known, that figure is considered together with the values of the other assets and liabilities. What does the court do next?[1]

7.11 As was pointed out above, pensions are part of the overall exercise to be performed under of s 25 of MCA 1973. It has been said on many occasions that there is no intrinsic reason why the property rights of the parties should be disturbed; redistribution in itself is not the purpose of the legislation, and it is necessary to find some reason, based on one or more of the circumstances of the case, to justify redistribution. The discretionary power of the court to adjust capital shares between the parties should not be exercised unless there is a manifest need to for intervention upon the application of the s 25 criteria.[2] This point was reinforced as to pensions by Singer J in the case referred to at **7.2** and **7.3** above. It must follow that any adjustment of a party's pension rights must be justified by some need on the part of the other party and not because of some perceived 'right to compensation'.

7.12 Assuming that the husband in most cases is the pension scheme member and that the wife has little or no pension provision, most cases will be approached on the basis of first considering whether or not the wife's reasonable needs include a need for pension provision. It is submitted that this is normally by no means the most pressing need, and the need for housing for the wife, and any dependent children, and her need for income would have been considered as the first priorities. However, assuming those needs to have been met, either from the wife's own resources or from redistribution of the assets, the pension position must be considered. Adjustment of pension rights obviously occurs only when one of the parties (assume it is the husband) has acquired some pension. This

---

1 In what follows, the author has come, by a different route, to roughly the same conclusions as those contained in an article entitled 'Pensions on divorce – compensation or needs?' by Catherine Hallam and David Salter in [1997] Fam Law 608. A careful reading of that article is recommended.

2 *H v H (Financial Provision: Capital Allowance)* [1993] 2 FLR 335 per Thorpe J.

point may seem too obvious to labour, but it is difficult to conceive of a case, except perhaps where the parties are very wealthy, in which need for pension would be considered in the abstract and without there being any pension assets to adjust.

7.13 It is therefore assumed that in the kind of case in which pensions are relevant, the husband has some pension rights. It must further be assumed that his own needs for housing, income etc have been met; in most cases, it would clearly be wrong, for example, to provide the funds for the wife to rehouse herself, leaving the husband with no adequate provision for housing and then to seek to attack his pension which might be the only asset or security he had left. Given those assumptions, the pension needs of the wife would have to be considered. In considering these, the following questions would be relevant.

(1) How old is she? It seems to be generally accepted that the younger the parties (particularly the wife), and the longer the time before retirement, the less relevant is the pension issue. Quite how long this period has to be to make it irrelevant is debatable.[1] Clearly, a wife aged under 30, perhaps even under 35, would find it difficult to mount a successful attack on a husband's pension. Equally clearly, a wife aged over 50 would have little problem. Between those ages exists an area of uncertainty and potential for litigation.

(2) How old is the husband and how soon will the pension become payable? This question may be particularly relevant when there is a significant discrepancy in the parties' ages.

(3) In the light of all the circumstances of the case, what are the wife's reasonable needs? In the context of pensions, these needs might be subdivided into need for income after the retirement of the husband or after his death, and need for capital after his retirement or death. Where there is an order for periodical payments without limit, clearly there will be a need for a continuing source of income; this might be met by

---

1   See eg *H v H (Financial Provision: Capital Allowance)* [1993] 2 FLR 335 and *Hedges v Hedges* [1991] 1 FLR 196.

means of periodical payments or by a one-off capital payment. The position of the wife if the husband dies must be considered.

7.14 Having decided what are the needs of the wife, what is available must be considered; it is, of course, necessary to remember that the husband is entitled to a pension as well, so that his needs must be considered unless it seems that he will be able to provide adequately for himself from other assets. The needs of the wife might be met by one of the orders now to be considered.

Offsetting

7.15 Offsetting will be appropriate only where there are sufficient other assets to provide a fund to meet the wife's needs or such of her needs as it is reasonable to cater for in the context of the parties' overall financial position. Ideally, a *Duxbury* fund[1] which would be sufficient to provide the wife's income and capital needs for life would serve this purpose, but it may be that a less ambitious amount of money would suit individual cases. Offsetting might be appropriate where the parties are comparatively young so that the wife's lack of pension is not yet serious but, where the husband had some pension provision. Here, it might be thought wrong to interfere with his pension entitlement and, instead, the wife should have some additional capital to compensate for her lack of provision.

Earmarking for income purposes (s 25B(4))

7.16 Earmarking for income purposes would be appropriate where a pension in payment was, either now or at some time in the future, to be earmarked to provide periodical payments. In effect, this would be equivalent to an attachment of earnings order against the pension fund. Clearly, it would be inappropriate where the parties wished there to be a clean break. It would also be dependent on the husband surviving, since it would cease on his death. It would always be liable to variation in the event of a change of circumstances of either party.

---

1   See *B v B (Discovery: Financial Provision)* [1990] 2 FLR 180 per Ward J.

Earmarking for a capital sum (s 25B(4))

7.17 Earmarking for a capital sum would be the case where the wife was to receive a deferred lump sum from the husband's pension entitlement. It might be appropriate where there was insufficient capital when the s 23 order was made and the only way to secure the money was from the pension fund. It would suffer from similar defects to an income order, particularly the fact that it may be varied, save that it would be possible to have a clean break.

Capital from commuted lump sum benefits (s 25B(7))

7.18 Capital from commuted lump sum benefits is, in effect, a device to secure a deferred lump sum and to compel the husband to make the capital fund available.

Earmarking of death-in-service benefits (s 25C(2)(a))

7.19 Earmarking of death-in-service benefits would be appropriate where the wife was financially dependent on the husband, either for her own periodical payments or for payments in respect of the children (whether direct or through the CSA). On the death of the husband before retirement, any lump sum payable on his death, or part thereof, would be paid to the wife. By s 25C(2)(b), the husband could be compelled to nominate the wife as the person to receive all or part of the benefits, and, by s 25C(2)(c), any trust of a retirement annuity contract could be overriden to secure payment for the wife. This class of order is also liable to be varied.

A pension sharing order

7.20 A pension sharing order would be most appropriate where it was intended that the parties should have a clean break and it was thought desirable to provide the wife with a share of the husband's pension entitlement to give her her own pension fund, or the base for such a fund. It would be possible for there to be a periodical payments order in addition to a pension sharing order in appropriate cases, but it would not be possible to make any form of earmarking order so that, for example, there could be no protection as to death-in-service benefits. The advantage of a pension sharing order would be that, subject to appeal, it could not be varied so that the pension credit transferred to the wife would be hers for life. There would be, therefore, certain advantages to a pension sharing order, but it might not be appropriate for a mother with young dependent children who wished to protect her income in the event of the husband's premature death. It would be highly appropriate for the wife who wanted a clean break in every sense of the term and wished to take her pension and go.

APPENDIX
Welfare Reform and Pensions Act 1999

(1999 c 30)

ARRANGEMENT OF SECTIONS

...

PART III

PENSIONS ON DIVORCE ETC.

PART IV

PENSION SHARING

CHAPTER I

SHARING OF RIGHTS UNDER PENSION ARRANGEMENTS

Pension sharing mechanism

Pension debits

Pension credits

Treatment of pension credit rights under schemes

Indexation

Charges by pension arrangements

CHAPTER II

SHARING OF STATE SCHEME RIGHTS

. . .

An Act to make provision about pensions and social security; to make provision for reducing under-occupation of dwellings by housing benefit claimants; to authorise certain expenditure by the Secretary of State having responsibility for social security; and for connected purposes. [11th November 1999]

...

PART III

PENSIONS ON DIVORCE ETC.

Pension sharing orders

19 Orders in England and Wales

Schedule 3 (which amends the Matrimonial Causes Act 1973 for the purpose of enabling the court to make pension sharing orders in connection with proceedings in England and Wales for divorce or nullity of marriage, and for supplementary purposes) shall have effect.

20 Orders in Scotland

(1) The Family Law (Scotland) Act 1985 shall be amended as follows.

(2) In section 8(1) (orders for financial provision), after paragraph (b) there shall be inserted—

'(baa) a pension sharing order.'

(3) In section 27 (interpretation), in subsection (1), there shall be inserted at the appropriate place—

' "pension sharing order" is an order which—
    (a) provides that one party's—
        (i)   shareable rights under a specified pension arrangement, or
        (ii) shareable state scheme rights,
        be subject to pension sharing for the benefit of the other party, and
    (b) specifies the percentage value, or the amount, to be transferred;'.

(4) In that section, after subsection (1) there shall be inserted—

'(1A) In subsection (1), in the definition of "pension sharing order"—

    (a) the reference to shareable rights under a pension arrangement is to rights in relation to which pension sharing is available under Chapter I of Part IV of the Welfare Reform and Pensions Act 1999, or under corresponding Northern Ireland legislation, and (b)　the reference to shareable state scheme rights is to rights in relation to which pension sharing is available under Chapter II of Part IV of the Welfare Reform and Pensions Act 1999, or under corresponding Northern Ireland legislation.'

Sections 25B to 25D of the Matrimonial Causes Act 1973

21　Amendments

Schedule 4 (which amends the sections about pensions inserted in the Matrimonial Causes Act 1973 by section 166 of the Pensions Act 1995) shall have effect.

22　Extension to overseas divorces etc.

(1) Part III of the Matrimonial and Family Proceedings Act 1984 (financial relief in England and Wales after overseas divorce etc.) shall be amended as follows.

(2) In section 18 (matters to which the court is to have regard in exercising its powers to make orders for financial relief), after subsection (3) there shall be inserted—

'(3A) The matters to which the court is to have regard under subsection (3) above—

(a)　so far as relating to paragraph (a) of section 25(2) of the 1973 Act, include any benefits under a pension arrangement which a party to the marriage has or is likely to have (whether or not in the foreseeable future), and

(b)　so far as relating to paragraph (h) of that provision, include any benefits under a pension arrangement which, by reason of the dissolution or annulment of the marriage, a party to the marriage will lose the chance of acquiring.'

(3) In that section, at the end there shall be added—

'(7) In this section—

(a)　"pension arrangement" has the meaning given by section 25D(3) of the 1973 Act, and

(b)　references to benefits under a pension arrangement include any benefits by way of pension, whether under a pension arrangement or not.'

(4) In section 21 (application of provisions of Part II of the Matrimonial Causes Act 1973), the existing provision shall become subsection (1) and, in that subsection, after paragraph (b) there shall be inserted—

> '(bd)   section 25B(3) to (7B) (power, by financial provision order, to attach payments under a pension arrangement, or to require the exercise of a right of commutation under such an arrangement);
> (be)   section 25C (extension of lump sum powers in relation to death benefits under a pension arrangement);'.

(5) In that section, after subsection (1) there shall be inserted—

> '(2) Subsection (1)(bd) and (be) above shall not apply where the court has jurisdiction to entertain an application for an order for financial relief by reason only of the situation in England or Wales of a dwelling-house which was a matrimonial home of the parties.

> (3) Section 25D(1) of the 1973 Act (effect of transfers on orders relating to rights under a pension arrangement) shall apply in relation to an order made under section 17 above by virtue of subsection (1)(bd) or (be) above as it applies in relation to an order made under section 23 of that Act by virtue of section 25B or 25C of the 1973 Act.

> (4) The Lord Chancellor may by regulations make for the purposes of this Part of this Act provision corresponding to any provision which may be made by him under subsections (2) to (2B) of section 25D of the 1973 Act.

> (5) Power to make regulations under this section shall be exercisable by statutory instrument which shall be subject to annulment in pursuance of a resolution of either House of Parliament.'

Miscellaneous

23   Supply of pension information in connection with divorce etc.

(1) The Secretary of State may by regulations—

  (a)   make provision imposing on the person responsible for a pension arrangement, or on the Secretary of State, requirements with respect to the supply of information relevant to any power with respect to—
    (i)   financial relief under Part II of the Matrimonial Causes Act 1973 or Part III of the Matrimonial and Family Proceedings Act 1984 (England and Wales powers in relation to domestic and overseas divorce etc.),

       (ii)   financial provision under the Family Law (Scotland) Act 1985 or Part IV of the Matrimonial and Family Proceedings Act 1984 (corresponding Scottish powers), or

       (iii)   financial relief under Part III of the Matrimonial Causes (Northern Ireland) Order 1978 or Part IV of the Matrimonial and Family Proceedings (Northern Ireland) Order 1989 (corresponding Northern Ireland powers);

  (b)   make provision about calculation and verification in relation to the valuation of—

       (i)   benefits under a pension arrangement, or

       (ii)   shareable state scheme rights,

for the purposes of regulations under paragraph (a)(i) or (iii);

  (c)   make provision about calculation and verification in relation to—

       (i)   the valuation of shareable rights under a pension arrangement or shareable state scheme rights for the purposes of regulations under paragraph (a)(ii), so far as relating to the making of orders for financial provision (within the meaning of the Family Law (Scotland) Act 1985), or

       (ii)   the valuation of benefits under a pension arrangement for the purposes of such regulations, so far as relating to the making of orders under section 12A of that Act;

  (d)   make provision for the purpose of enabling the person responsible for a pension arrangement to recover prescribed charges in respect of providing information in accordance with regulations under paragraph (a).

(2) Regulations under subsection (1)(b) or (c) may include provision for calculation or verification in accordance with guidance from time to time prepared by a person prescribed by the regulations.

(3) Regulations under subsection (1)(d) may include provision for the application in prescribed circumstances, with or without modification, of any provision made by virtue of section 41(2).

(4) In subsection (1)—

  (a)   the reference in paragraph (c)(i) to shareable rights under a pension arrangement is to rights in relation to which pension sharing is available under Chapter I of Part IV, or under corresponding Northern Ireland legislation, and

  (b)   the references to shareable state scheme rights are to rights in relation to which pension sharing is available under Chapter II of Part IV, or under corresponding Northern Ireland legislation.

24   Charges by pension arrangements in relation to earmarking orders

The Secretary of State may by regulations make provision for the purpose of enabling the person responsible for a pension arrangement to recover prescribed charges in respect of complying with—

(a)   an order under section 23 of the Matrimonial Causes Act 1973 (financial provision orders in connection with divorce etc.), so far as it includes provision made by virtue of section 25B or 25C of that Act (powers to include provision about pensions),

(b)   an order under section 12A(2) or (3) of the Family Law (Scotland) Act 1985 (powers in relation to pensions lump sums when making a capital sum order), or

(c)   an order under Article 25 of the Matrimonial Causes (Northern Ireland) Order 1978, so far as it includes provision made by virtue of Article 27B or 27C of that Order (Northern Ireland powers corresponding to those mentioned in paragraph (a)).

Supplementary

25   Power to make consequential amendments of Part III

(1) If any amendment by the Family Law Act 1996 of Part II or IV of the Matrimonial Causes Act 1973 comes into force before the day on which any provision of this Part comes into force, the Lord Chancellor may by order make such consequential amendment of that provision as he thinks fit.

(2) No order under this section may be made unless a draft of the order has been laid before and approved by resolution of each House of Parliament.

26   Interpretation of Part III

(1) In this Part—

'occupational pension scheme' has the same meaning as in the Pension Schemes Act 1993;

'pension arrangement' means

(a)   an occupational pension scheme,
(b)   a personal pension scheme,
(c)   a retirement annuity contract,
(d)   an annuity or insurance policy purchased, or transferred, for the purpose of giving effect to rights under an occupational pension scheme or a personal pension scheme, and

(e) an annuity purchased, or entered into, for the purpose of discharging liability in respect of a pension credit under section 29(1)(b) or under corresponding Northern Ireland legislation;

'personal pension scheme' has the same meaning as in the Pension Schemes Act 1993;

'prescribed' means prescribed by regulations made by the Secretary of State;

'retirement annuity contract' means a contract or scheme approved under Chapter III of Part XIV of the Income and Corporation Taxes Act 1988;

'trustees or managers', in relation to an occupational pension scheme or a personal pension scheme, means—

(a) in the case of a scheme established under a trust, the trustees of the scheme, and
(b) in any other case, the managers of the scheme.

(2) References to the person responsible for a pension arrangement are—

(a) in the case of an occupational pension scheme or a personal pension scheme, to the trustees or managers of the scheme,
(b) in the case of a retirement annuity contract or an annuity falling within paragraph (d) or (e) of the definition of 'pension arrangement' above, the provider of the annuity, and
(c) in the case of an insurance policy falling within paragraph (d) of the definition of that expression, the insurer.

PART IV

PENSION SHARING

CHAPTER I

SHARING OF RIGHTS UNDER PENSION ARRANGEMENTS

Pension sharing mechanism

27 Scope of mechanism

(1) Pension sharing is available under this Chapter in relation to a person's shareable rights under any pension arrangement other than an excepted public service pension scheme.

(2) For the purposes of this Chapter, a person's shareable rights under a pension arrangement are any rights of his under the arrangement, other than rights of a description specified by regulations made by the Secretary of State.

(3) For the purposes of subsection (1), a public service pension scheme is excepted if it is specified by order made by such Minister of the Crown or government department as may be designated by the Treasury as having responsibility for the scheme.

28   Activation of pension sharing

(1) Section 29 applies on the taking effect of any of the following relating to a person's shareable rights under a pension arrangement—

(a)   a pension sharing order under the Matrimonial Causes Act 1973,

(b)   provision which corresponds to the provision which may be made by such an order and which—
  (i)   is contained in a qualifying agreement between the parties to a marriage, and
  (ii) takes effect on the dissolution of the marriage under the Family Law Act 1996,

(c)   provision which corresponds to the provision which may be made by such an order and which—
  (i)   is contained in a qualifying agreement between the parties to a marriage or former marriage, and
  (ii) takes effect after the dissolution of the marriage under the Family Law Act 1996,

(d)   an order under Part III of the Matrimonial and Family Proceedings Act 1984 (financial relief in England and Wales in relation to overseas divorce etc.) corresponding to such an order as is mentioned in paragraph (a),

(e)   a pension sharing order under the Family Law (Scotland) Act 1985,

(f)   provision which corresponds to the provision which may be made by such an order and which—
  (i)   is contained in a qualifying agreement between the parties to a marriage,
  (ii)   is in such form as the Secretary of State may prescribe by regulations, and
  (iii) takes effect on the grant, in relation to the marriage, of decree of divorce under the Divorce (Scotland) Act 1976 or of declarator of nullity,

(g) an order under Part IV of the Matrimonial and Family Proceedings Act 1984 (financial relief in Scotland in relation to overseas divorce etc.) corresponding to such an order as is mentioned in paragraph (e),

(h) a pension sharing order under Northern Ireland legislation, and

(i) an order under Part IV of the Matrimonial and Family Proceedings (Northern Ireland) Order 1989 (financial relief in Northern Ireland in relation to overseas divorce etc.) corresponding to such an order as is mentioned in paragraph (h).

(2) For the purposes of subsection (1)(b) and (c), a qualifying agreement is one which—

(a) has been entered into in such circumstances as the Lord Chancellor may prescribe by regulations, and

(b) satisfies such requirements as the Lord Chancellor may so prescribe.

(3) For the purposes of subsection (1)(f), a qualifying agreement is one which—

(a) has been entered into in such circumstances as the Secretary of State may prescribe by regulations, and

(b) is registered in the Books of Council and Session.

(4) Subsection (1)(b) does not apply if—

(a) the pension arrangement to which the provision relates is the subject of a pension sharing order under the Matrimonial Causes Act 1973 in relation to the marriage, or

(b) there is in force a requirement imposed by virtue of section 25B or 25C of that Act (powers to include in financial provision orders requirements relating to benefits under pension arrangements) which relates to benefits or future benefits to which the party who is the transferor is entitled under the pension arrangement to which the provision relates.

(5) Subsection (1)(c) does not apply if—

(a) the marriage was dissolved by an order under section 3 of the Family Law Act 1996 (divorce not preceded by separation) and the satisfaction of the requirements of section 9(2) of that Act (settlement of future financial arrangements) was a precondition to the making of the order,

(b) the pension arrangement to which the provision relates—

(i) is the subject of a pension sharing order under the Matrimonial Causes Act 1973 in relation to the marriage, or

(ii) has already been the subject of pension sharing between the parties, or

(c) there is in force a requirement imposed by virtue of section 25B or 25C of that Act which relates to benefits or future benefits to which the party who is the transferor is entitled under the pension arrangement to which the provision relates.

(6) Subsection (1)(f) does not apply if there is in force an order under section 12A(2) or (3) of the Family Law (Scotland) Act 1985 which relates to benefits or future benefits to which the party who is the transferor is entitled under the pension arrangement to which the provision relates.

(7) For the purposes of this section, an order or provision falling within subsection (1)(e), (f) or (g) shall be deemed never to have taken effect if the person responsible for the arrangement to which the order or provision relates does not receive before the end of the period of 2 months beginning with the relevant date—

(a) copies of the relevant matrimonial documents, and

(b) such information relating to the transferor and transferee as the Secretary of State may prescribe by regulations under section 34(1)(b)(ii).

(8) The relevant date for the purposes of subsection (7) is—

(a) in the case of an order or provision falling within subsection (1)(e) or (f), the date of the extract of the decree or declarator responsible for the divorce or annulment to which the order or provision relates, and

(b) in the case of an order falling within subsection (1)(g), the date of disposal of the application under section 28 of the Matrimonial and Family Proceedings Act 1984.

(9) The reference in subsection (7)(a) to the relevant matrimonial documents is—

(a) in the case of an order falling within subsection (1)(e) or (g), to copies of the order and the order, decree or declarator responsible for the divorce or annulment to which it relates, and

(b) in the case of provision falling within subsection (1)(f), to—

(i) copies of the provision and the order, decree or declarator responsible for the divorce or annulment to which it relates, and

(ii) documentary evidence that the agreement containing the provision is one to which subsection (3)(a) applies.

(10) The sheriff may, on the application of any person having an interest, make an order—

(a) extending the period of 2 months referred to in subsection (7), and

(b) if that period has already expired, providing that, if the person responsible for the arrangement receives the documents and information concerned before the end of the period specified in the order, subsection (7) is to be treated as never having applied.

(11) In subsections (4)(b), (5)(c) and (6), the reference to the party who is the transferor is to the party to whose rights the provision relates.

29   Creation of pension debits and credits

(1) On the application of this section—

(a) the transferor's shareable rights under the relevant arrangement become subject to a debit of the appropriate amount, and

(b) the transferee becomes entitled to a credit of that amount as against the person responsible for that arrangement.

(2) Where the relevant order or provision specifies a percentage value to be transferred, the appropriate amount for the purposes of subsection (1) is the specified percentage of the cash equivalent of the relevant benefits on the valuation day.

(3) Where the relevant order or provision specifies an amount to be transferred, the appropriate amount for the purposes of subsection (1) is the lesser of—

(a) the specified amount, and

(b) the cash equivalent of the relevant benefits on the valuation day.

(4) Where the relevant arrangement is an occupational pension scheme and the transferor is in pensionable service under the scheme on the transfer day, the relevant benefits for the purposes of subsections (2) and (3) are the benefits or future benefits to which he would be entitled under the scheme by virtue of his shareable rights under it had his pensionable service terminated immediately before that day.

(5) Otherwise, the relevant benefits for the purposes of subsections (2) and (3) are the benefits or future benefits to which, immediately before the transfer day, the transferor is entitled under the terms of the relevant arrangement by virtue of his shareable rights under it.

(6) The Secretary of State may by regulations provide for any description of benefit to be disregarded for the purposes of subsection (4) or (5).

(7) For the purposes of this section, the valuation day is such day within the implementation period for the credit under subsection (1)(b) as the person responsible for the relevant arangement may specify by notice in writing to the transferor and transferee.

(8) In this section—

'relevant arrangement' means the arrangement to which the relevant order or provision relates;

'relevant order or provision' means the order or provision by virtue of which this section applies;

'transfer day' means the day on which the relevant order or provision takes effect;

'transferor' means the person to whose rights the relevant order or provision relates;

'transferee' means the person for whose benefit the relevant order or provision is made.

30　Cash equivalents

(1) The Secretary of State may by regulations make provision about the calculation and verification of cash equivalents for the purposes of section 29.

(2) The power conferred by subsection (1) includes power to provide for calculation or verification—

- (a) in such manner as may, in the particular case, be approved by a person prescribed by the regulations, or
- (b) in accordance with guidance from time to time prepared by a person so prescribed.

Pension debits

31　Reduction of benefit

(1) Subject to subsection (2), where a person's shareable rights under a pension arrangement are subject to a pension debit, each benefit or future benefit—

- (a) to which he is entitled under the arrangement by virtue of those rights, and

(b)   which is a qualifying benefit,

is reduced by the appropriate percentage.

(2) Where a pension debit relates to the shareable rights under an occupational pension scheme of a person who is in pensionable service under the scheme on the transfer day, each benefit or future benefit—

(a)   to which the person is entitled under the scheme by virtue of those rights, and
(b)   which corresponds to a qualifying benefit,

is reduced by an amount equal to the appropriate percentage of the corresponding qualifying benefit.

(3) A benefit is a qualifying benefit for the purposes of subsections (1) and (2) if the cash equivalent by reference to which the amount of the pension debit is determined includes an amount in respect of it.

(4) The provisions of this section override any provision of a pension arrangement to which they apply to the extent that the provision conflicts with them.

(5) In this section—

'appropriate percentage', in relation to a pension debit, means—

(a)   if the relevant order or provision specifies the percentage value to be transferred, that percentage;
(b)   if the relevant order or provision specifies an amount to be transferred, the percentage which the appropriate amount for the purposes of subsection (1) of section 29 represents of the amount mentioned in subsection (3)(b) of that section;

'relevant order or provision', in relation to a pension debit, means the pension sharing order or provision on which the debit depends;

'transfer day', in relation to a pension debit, means the day on which the relevant order or provision takes effect.

32   Effect on contracted-out rights

(1) The Pension Schemes Act 1993 shall be amended as follows.

(2) In section 10 (protected rights), in subsection (1), for 'subsections (2) and (3)' there shall be substituted 'the following provisions of this section', and at the end there shall be added—

'(4) Where, in the case of a scheme which makes such provision as is mentioned in subsection (2) or (3), a member's rights under the scheme become subject to a pension debit, his protected rights shall exclude the appropriate percentage of the rights which were his protected rights immediately before the day on which the pension debit arose.

(5) For the purposes of subsection (4), the appropriate percentage is—

    (a)   if the order or provision on which the pension debit depends specifies the percentage value to be transferred, that percentage;

    (b)   if the order or provision on which the pension debit depends specifies an amount to be transferred, the percentage which the appropriate amount for the purposes of subsection (1) of section 29 of the Welfare Reform and Pensions Act 1999 (lesser of specified amount and cash equivalent of transferor's benefits) represents of the amount mentioned in subsection (3)(b) of that section (cash equivalent of transferor's benefits).'

(3) After section 15 there shall be inserted—

'15A Reduction of guaranteed minimum in consequence of pension debit

(1) Where—

    (a)   an earner has a guaranteed minimum in relation to the pension provided by a scheme, and

    (b)   his right to the pension becomes subject to a pension debit,

his guaranteed minimum in relation to the scheme is, subject to subsection (2), reduced by the appropriate percentage.

(2) Where the earner is in pensionable service under the scheme on the day on which the order or provision on which the pension debit depends takes effect, his guaranteed minimum in relation to the scheme is reduced by an amount equal to the appropriate percentage of the corresponding qualifying benefit.

(3) For the purposes of subsection (2), the corresponding qualifying benefit is the guaranteed minimum taken for the purpose of calculating the cash equivalent by reference to which the amount of the pension debit is determined.

(4) For the purposes of this section the appropriate percentage is—

    (a)   if the order or provision on which the pension debit depends specifies the percentage value to be transferred, that percentage;

    (b)   if the order or provision on which the pension debit depends specifies an amount to be transferred, the percentage which the appropriate amount for the purposes of subsection (1) of section 29 of the Welfare Reform and Pensions Act 1999 (lesser of specified amount and cash equivalent of transferor's benefits) represents of the amount mentioned in subsection (3)(b) of that section (cash equivalent of transferor's benefits).'

(4) In section 47 (entitlement to guaranteed minimum pensions for the purposes of the relationship with social security benefits), at the end there shall be added—

'(6) For the purposes of section 46, a person shall be treated as entitled to any guaranteed minimum pension to which he would have been entitled but for any reduction under section 15A.'

(5) In section 181(1), there shall be inserted at the appropriate place—

' "pension debit" means a debit under section 29(1)(a) of the Welfare Reform and Pensions Act 1999;'.

Pension credits

33   Time for discharge of liability

(1) A person subject to liability in respect of a pension credit shall discharge his liability before the end of the implementation period for the credit.

(2) Where the trustees or managers of an occupational pension scheme have not done what is required to discharge their liability in respect of a pension credit before the end of the implementation period for the credit—

    (a)   they shall, except in such cases as the Secretary of State may prescribe by regulations, notify the Regulatory Authority of that fact within such period as the Secretary of State may so prescribe, and

    (b)   section 10 of the Pensions Act 1995 (power of the Regulatory Authority to impose civil penalties) shall apply to any trustee or manager who has failed to take all such steps as are reasonable to ensure that liability in respect of the credit was discharged before the end of the implementation period for it.

(3) If trustees or managers to whom subsection (2)(a) applies fail to perform the obligation imposed by that provision, section 10 of the Pensions Act 1995 shall apply to any trustee or manager who has failed to take all reasonable steps to ensure that the obligation was performed.

(4) On the application of the trustees or managers of an occupational pension scheme who are subject to liability in respect of a pension credit, the Regulatory Authority may extend the implementation period for the credit for the purposes of this section if it is satisfied that the application is made in such circumstances as the Secretary of State may prescribe by regulations.

(5) In this section 'the Regulatory Authority' means the Occupational Pensions Regulatory Authority.

34 'Implementation period'

(1) For the purposes of this Chapter, the implementation period for a pension credit is the period of 4 months beginning with the later of—

  (a) the day on which the relevant order or provision takes effect, and
  (b) the first day on which the person responsible for the pension arrangement to which the relevant order or provision relates is in receipt of—

  (i)   the relevant matrimonial documents, and
  (ii) such information relating to the transferor and transferee as the Secretary of State may prescribe by regulations.

(2) The reference in subsection (1)(b)(i) to the relevant matrimonial documents is to copies of—

  (a) the relevant order or provision, and
  (b) the order, decree or declarator responsible for the divorce or annulment to which it relates,

and, if the pension credit depends on provision falling within subsection (1)(f) of section 28, to documentary evidence that the agreement containing the provision is one to which subsection (3)(a) of that section applies.

(3) Subsection (1) is subject to any provision made by regulations under section 41(2)(a).

(4) The Secretary of State may by regulations—

  (a) make provision requiring a person subject to liability in respect of a pension credit to notify the transferor and transferee of the day on which the implementation period for the credit begins;

(b) provide for this section to have effect with modifications where the pension arrangement to which the relevant order or provision relates is being wound up;

(c) provide for this section to have effect with modifications where the pension credit depends on a pension sharing order and the order is the subject of an application for leave to appeal out of time.

(5) In this section—

'relevant order or provision', in relation to a pension credit, means the pension sharing order or provision on which the pension credit depends;

'transferor' means the person to whose rights the relevant order or provision relates;

'transferee' means the person for whose benefit the relevant order or provision is made.

35   Mode of discharge of liability

(1) Schedule 5 (which makes provision about how liability in respect of a pension credit may be discharged) shall have effect.

(2) Where the person entitled to a pension credit dies before liability in respect of the credit has been discharged—

(a) Schedule 5 shall cease to have effect in relation to the discharge of liability in respect of the credit, and

(b) liability in respect of the credit shall be discharged in accordance with regulations made by the Secretary of State.

Treatment of pension credit rights under schemes

36   Safeguarded rights

After section 68 of the Pension Schemes Act 1993 there shall be inserted—

'PART IIIA

SAFEGUARDED RIGHTS

68A Safeguarded rights

(1) Subject to subsection (2), the safeguarded rights of a member of an occupational pension scheme or a personal pension scheme are such of his rights to future benefits under the scheme as are attributable

(directly or indirectly) to a pension credit in respect of which the reference rights are, or include, contracted-out rights or safeguarded rights.

(2) If the rules of an occupational pension scheme or a personal pension scheme so provide, a member's safeguarded rights are such of his rights falling within subsection (1) as—

(a) in the case of rights directly attributable to a pension credit, represent the safeguarded percentage of the rights acquired by virtue of the credit, and

(b) in the case of rights directly attributable to a transfer payment, represent the safeguarded percentage of the rights acquired by virtue of the payment.

(3) For the purposes of subsection (2)(a), the safeguarded percentage is the percentage of the rights by reference to which the amount of the credit is determined which are contracted-out rights or safeguarded rights.

(4) For the purposes of subsection (2)(b), the safeguarded percentage is the percentage of the rights in respect of which the transfer payment is made which are contracted-out rights or safeguarded rights.

(5) In this section—

"contracted-out rights" means such rights under, or derived from—

(a) an occupational pension scheme contracted-out by virtue of section 9(2) or (3), or

(b) an appropriate personal pension scheme,

as may be prescribed;

"reference rights", in relation to a pension credit, means the rights by reference to which the amount of the credit is determined.

68B Requirements relating to safeguarded rights

lations may prescribe requirements to be met in relation to safeguarded rights by an occupational pension scheme or a personal pension scheme.

68C   Reserve powers in relation to non-complying schemes

(1) This section applies to—

- (a)   any occupational pension scheme, other than a public service pension scheme, and
- (b)   any personal pension scheme.

(2) If any scheme to which this section applies does not comply with a requirement prescribed under section 68B and there are any persons who—

- (a)   have safeguarded rights under the scheme, or
- (b)   are entitled to any benefit giving effect to such rights under the scheme,

the Inland Revenue may direct the trustees or managers of the scheme to take or refrain from taking such steps as they may specify in writing for the purpose of safeguarding the rights of persons falling within paragraph (a) or (b).

(3) A direction under subsection (2) shall be final and binding on the trustees or managers to whom the direction is given and any person claiming under them.

(4) An appeal on a point of law shall lie to the High Court or, in Scotland, the Court of Session from a direction under subsection (2) at the instance of the trustees or managers, or any person claiming under them.

(5) A direction under subsection (2) shall be enforceable—

- (a)   in England and Wales, in a county court, as if it were an order of that court, and
- (b)   in Scotland, by the sheriff, as if it were an order of the sheriff and whether or not the sheriff could himself have given such an order.

68D   Power to control transfer or discharge of liability

Regulations may prohibit or restrict the transfer or discharge of any liability under an occupational pension scheme or a personal pension scheme in respect of safeguarded rights except in prescribed circumstances or on prescribed conditions.'

37   Requirements relating to pension credit benefit

After section 101 of the Pension Schemes Act 1993 there shall be inserted—

'PART IVA

REQUIREMENTS RELATING TO PENSION CREDIT BENEFIT

CHAPTER I

PENSION CREDIT BENEFIT UNDER OCCUPATIONAL SCHEMES

101A   Scope of Chapter I

(1) This Chapter applies to any occupational pension scheme whose resources are derived in whole or part from—

    (a)   payments to which subsection (2) applies made or to be made by one or more employers of earners to whom the scheme applies, or

    (b)   such other payments by the earner or his employer, or both, as may be prescribed for different categories of scheme.

(2) This subsection applies to payments—

    (a)   under an actual or contingent legal obligation, or

    (b)   in the exercise of a power conferred, or the discharge of a duty imposed, on a Minister of the Crown, government department or any other person, being a power or duty which extends to the disbursement or allocation of public money.

101B   Interpretation

In this Chapter—

"scheme" means an occupational pension scheme to which this Chapter applies;

"pension credit rights" means rights to future benefits under a scheme which are attributable (directly or indirectly) to a pension credit;

"pension credit benefit", in relation to a scheme, means the benefits payable under the scheme to or in respect of a person by virtue of rights under the scheme attributable (directly or indirectly) to a pension credit;

"normal benefit age", in relation to a scheme, means the earliest age at which a person who has pension credit rights under the scheme is entitled to receive a pension by virtue of those rights (disregarding any scheme rule making special provision as to early payment of pension on grounds of ill-health or otherwise).

101C Basic principle as to pension credit benefit

(1) Normal benefit age under a scheme must be between 60 and 65.

(2) A scheme must not provide for payment of pension credit benefit in the form of a lump sum at any time before normal benefit age, except in such circumstances as may be prescribed.

101D Form of pension credit benefit and its alternatives

(1) Subject to subsection (2) and section 101E, a person's pension credit benefit under a scheme must be—

   (a)   payable directly out of the resources of the scheme, or
   (b)   assured to him by such means as may be prescribed.

(2) Subject to subsections (3) and (4), a scheme may, instead of providing a person's pension credit benefit, provide—

   (a)   for his pension credit rights under the scheme to be transferred to another occupational pension scheme or a personal pension scheme with a view to acquiring rights for him under the rules of the scheme, or
   (b)   for such alternatives to pension credit benefit as may be prescribed.

(3) The option conferred by subsection (2)(a) is additional to any obligation imposed by Chapter II of this Part.

(4) The alternatives specified in subsection (2)(a) and (b) may only be by way of complete or partial substitute for pension credit benefit—

   (a)   if the person entitled to the benefit consents, or
   (b)   in such other cases as may be prescribed.

101E Discharge of liability where pension credit or alternative benefits secured by insurance policies or annuity contracts

(1) A transaction to which section 19 applies discharges the trustees or managers of a scheme from their liability to provide pension credit

benefit or any alternative to pension credit benefit for or in respect of a member of the scheme if and to the extent that—

 (a) it results in pension credit benefit, or any alternative to pension credit benefit, for or in respect of the member being appropriately secured (within the meaning of that section),

 (b) the transaction is entered into with the consent of the member or, if the member has died, of the member's widow or widower, and

 (c) such requirements as may be prescribed are met.

(2) Regulations may provide that subsection (1)(b) shall not apply in prescribed circumstances.

CHAPTER II

TRANSFER VALUES

101F Power to give transfer notice

(1) An eligible member of a qualifying scheme may by notice in writing require the trustees or managers of the scheme to use an amount equal to the cash equivalent of his pension credit benefit for such one or more of the authorised purposes as he may specify in the notice.

(2) In the case of a member of an occupational pension scheme, the authorised purposes are—

 (a) to acquire rights allowed under the rules of an occupational pension scheme, or personal pension scheme, which is an eligible scheme,

 (b) to purchase from one or more insurance companies such as are mentioned in section 19(4)(a), chosen by the member and willing to accept payment on account of the member from the trustees or managers, one or more annuities which satisfy the prescribed requirements, and

 (c) in such circumstances as may be prescribed, to subscribe to other pension arrangements which satisfy prescribed requirements.

(3) In the case of a member of a personal pension scheme, the authorised purposes are—

(a) to acquire rights allowed under the rules of an occupational pension scheme, or personal pension scheme, which is an eligible scheme, and

(b) in such circumstances as may be prescribed, to subscribe to other pension arrangements which satisfy prescribed requirements.

(4) The cash equivalent for the purposes of subsection (1) shall—

(a) in the case of a salary related occupational pension scheme, be taken to be the amount shown in the relevant statement under section 101H, and

(b) in any other case, be determined by reference to the date the notice under that subsection is given.

(5) The requirements which may be prescribed under subsection (2) or (3) include, in particular, requirements of the Inland Revenue.

(6) In subsections (2) and (3), references to an eligible scheme are to a scheme—

(a) the trustees or managers of which are able and willing to accept payment in respect of the member's pension credit rights, and

(b) which satisfies the prescribed requirements.

(7) In this Chapter, "transfer notice" means a notice under subsection (1).

101G Restrictions on power to give transfer notice

(1) In the case of a salary related occupational pension scheme, the power to give a transfer notice may only be exercised if—

(a) the member has been provided with a statement under section 101H, and

(b) not more than 3 months have passed since the date by reference to which the amount shown in the statement is determined.

(2) The power to give a transfer notice may not be exercised in the case of an occupational pension scheme if—

(a) there is less than a year to go until the member reaches normal benefit age, or

(b) the pension to which the member is entitled by virtue of his pension credit rights, or benefit in lieu of that pension, or any part of it has become payable.

(3) Where an eligible member of a qualifying scheme—

(a) is entitled to make an application under section 95 to the trustees or managers of the scheme, or

(b) would be entitled to do so, but for the fact that he has not received a statement under section 93A in respect of which the guarantee date is sufficiently recent,

he may not, if the scheme so provides, exercise the power to give them a transfer notice unless he also makes an application to them under section 95.

(4) The power to give a transfer notice may not be exercised if a previous transfer notice given by the member to the trustees or managers of the scheme is outstanding.

101H Salary related schemes: statements of entitlement

(1) The trustees or managers of a qualifying scheme which is a salary related occupational pension scheme shall, on the application of an eligible member, provide him with a written statement of the amount of the cash equivalent of his pension credit benefit under the scheme.

(2) For the purposes of subsection (1), the amount of the cash equivalent shall be determined by reference to a date falling within—

(a) the prescribed period beginning with the date of the application, and

(b) the prescribed period ending with the date on which the statement under that subsection is provided to the applicant.

(3) Regulations may make provision in relation to applications under subsection (1) and may, in particular, restrict the making of successive applications.

(4) If trustees or managers to whom subsection (1) applies fail to perform an obligation under that subsection, section 10 of the Pensions Act 1995 (power of the Regulatory Authority to impose civil penalties) shall apply to any trustee or manager who has failed to take all such steps as are reasonable to secure that the obligation was performed.

101I Calculation of cash equivalents

Cash equivalents for the purposes of this Chapter shall be calculated and verified in the prescribed manner.

101J Time for compliance with transfer notice

(1) Trustees or managers of a qualifying scheme who receive a transfer notice shall comply with the notice—

  (a) in the case of an occupational pension scheme, within 6 months of the valuation date or, if earlier, by the date on which the member to whom the notice relates reaches normal benefit age, and

  (b) in the case of a personal pension scheme, within 6 months of the date on which they receive the notice.

(2) The Regulatory Authority may, in prescribed circumstances, extend the period for complying with the notice.

(3) If the Regulatory Authority are satisfied—

  (a) that there has been a relevant change of circumstances since they granted an extension under subsection (2), or

  (b) that they granted an extension under that subsection in ignorance of a material fact or on the basis of a mistake as to a material fact,

they may revoke or reduce the extension.

(4) Where the trustees or managers of an occupational pension scheme have failed to comply with a transfer notice before the end of the period for compliance—

  (a) they shall, except in prescribed cases, notify the Regulatory Authority of that fact within the prescribed period, and

  (b) section 10 of the Pensions Act 1995 (power of the Regulatory Authority to impose civil penalties) shall apply to any trustee or manager who has failed to take all such steps as are reasonable to ensure that the notice was complied with before the end of the period for compliance.

(5) If trustees or managers to whom subsection (4)(a) applies fail to perform the obligation imposed by that provision, section 10 of the Pensions Act 1995 shall apply to any trustee or manager who has failed to take all such steps as are reasonable to ensure that the obligation was performed.

(6) Regulations may—

  (a) make provision in relation to applications under subsection (2), and

(b) provide that subsection (4) shall not apply in prescribed circumstances.

(7) In this section, "valuation date", in relation to a transfer notice given to the trustees or managers of an occupational pension scheme, means—

(a) in the case of a salary related scheme, the date by reference to which the amount shown in the relevant statement under section 101H is determined, and
(b) in the case of any other scheme, the date the notice is given.

101K   Withdrawal of transfer notice

(1) Subject to subsections (2) and (3), a person who has given a transfer notice may withdraw it by giving the trustees or managers to whom it was given notice in writing that he no longer requires them to comply with it.

(2) A transfer notice may not be withdrawn if the trustees or managers have already entered into an agreement with a third party to use the whole or part of the amount they are required to use in accordance with the notice.

(3) If the giving of a transfer notice depended on the making of an application under section 95, the notice may only be withdrawn if the application is also withdrawn.

101L   Variation of the amount required to be used

(1) Regulations may make provision for the amount required to be used under section 101F(1) to be increased or reduced in prescribed circumstances.

(2) Without prejudice to the generality of subsection (1), the circumstances which may be prescribed include—

(a) failure by the trustees or managers of a qualifying scheme to comply with a notice under section 101F(1) within 6 months of the date by reference to which the amount of the cash equivalent falls to be determined, and
(b) the state of funding of a qualifying scheme.

(3) Regulations under subsection (1) may have the effect of extinguishing an obligation under section 101F(1).

101M   Effect of transfer on trustees' duties

Compliance with a transfer notice shall have effect to discharge the trustees or managers of a qualifying scheme from any obligation to provide the pension credit benefit of the eligible member who gave the notice.

101N   Matters to be disregarded in calculations

In making any calculation for the purposes of this Chapter—

(a)   any charge or lien on, and
(b)   any set-off against,

the whole or part of a pension shall be disregarded.

101O   Service of notices

A notice under section 101F(1) or 101K(1) shall be taken to have been given if it is delivered to the trustees or managers personally or sent by post in a registered letter or by recorded delivery service.

101P   Interpretation of Chapter II

(1) In this Chapter—

"eligible member", in relation to a qualifying scheme, means a member who has pension credit rights under the scheme;

"normal benefit age", in relation to an eligible member of a qualifying scheme, means the earliest age at which the member is entitled to receive a pension by virtue of his pension credit rights under the scheme (disregarding any scheme rule making special provision as to early payment of pension on grounds of ill-health or otherwise);

"pension credit benefit", in relation to an eligible member of a qualifying scheme, means the benefits payable under the scheme to or in respect of the member by virtue of rights under the scheme attributable (directly or indirectly) to a pension credit;

"pension credit rights", in relation to a qualifying scheme, means rights to future benefits under the scheme which are attributable (directly or indirectly) to a pension credit;

"qualifying scheme" means a funded occupational pension scheme and a personal pension scheme;

"transfer notice" has the meaning given by section 101F(7).

(2) For the purposes of this Chapter, an occupational pension scheme is salary related if—

(a) it is not a money purchase scheme, and
(b) it does not fall within a prescribed class.

(3) In this Chapter, references to the relevant statement under section 101H, in relation to a transfer notice given to the trustees or managers of a salary related occupational pension scheme, are to the statement under that section on which the giving of the notice depended.

(4) For the purposes of this section, an occupational pension scheme is funded if it meets its liabilities out of a fund accumulated for the purpose during the life of the scheme.

101Q   Power to modify Chapter II in relation to hybrid schemes

Regulations may apply to this Chapter with prescribed modifications to occupational pension schemes—

(a) which are not money purchase schemes, but
(b) where some of the benefits that may be provided are money purchase benefits.'

38   Treatment in winding up

(1) In section 73 of the Pensions Act 1995 (treatment of rights on winding up of an occupational pension scheme to which section 56 of that Act (minimum funding requirement) applies), in subsection (3) (classification of liabilities), in paragraph (c) (accrued rights), at the end of sub-paragraph (i) there shall be inserted—

'(ia) future pensions, or other future benefits, attributable (directly or indirectly) to pension credits (but excluding increases to pensions),'.

(2) In the case of an occupational pension scheme which is not a scheme to which section 56 of the Pensions Act 1995 applies, rights attributable (directly or indirectly) to a pension credit are to be accorded in a winding up the same treatment—

(a) if they have come into payment, as the rights of a pensioner member, and
(b) if they have not come into payment, as the rights of a deferred member.

(3) Subsection (2) overrides the provisions of a scheme to the extent that it conflicts with them, and the scheme has effect with such modifications as may be required in consequence.

(4) In subsection (2)—

(a) 'deferred member' and 'pensioner member' have the same meanings as in Part I of the Pensions Act 1995,

(b) 'pension credit' includes a credit under Northern Ireland legislation corresponding to section 29(1)(b), and

(c) references to rights attributable to a person credit having come into payment are to the person to whom the rights belong having become entitled by virtue of the rights to the present payment of pension or other benefits.

Indexation

39   Public service pension schemes

(1) The Pensions (Increase) Act 1971 shall be amended as follows.

(2) In section 3 (qualifying conditions), after subsection (2) there shall be inserted—

'(2A) A pension attributable to the pensioner having become entitled to a pension credit shall not be increased unless the pensioner has attained the age of fifty-five years.'

(3) In section 8, in subsection (1) (definition of 'pension'), in paragraph (a), the words from '(either' to 'person)' shall be omitted.

(4) In that section, in subsection (2) (when pension deemed for purposes of the Act to begin), after 'pension', in the first place, there shall be inserted 'which is not attributable to a pension credit', and after that subsection there shall be inserted—

'(2A) A pension which is attributable to a pension credit shall be deemed for purposes of this Act to begin on the day on which the order or provision on which the credit depends takes effect.'

(5) In section 17(1) (interpretation)—

(a) for the definitions of 'derivative pension' and 'principal pension' there shall be substituted—
'"derivative pension" means a pension which—

(a)   is not payable in respect of the pensioner's own services, and

(b)   is not attributable to the pensioner having become entitled to a pension credit;',

(b)   after the definition of 'pension' there shall be inserted—
'"pension credit" means a credit under section 29(1)(b) of the Welfare Reform and Pensions Act 1999 or under corresponding Northern Ireland legislation;
"principal pension" means a pension which—

(a)   is payable in respect of the pensioner's own services, or

(b)   is attributable to the pensioner having become entitled to a pension credit;', and

(c)   for the definition of 'widow's pension' there shall be substituted—
'"widow's pension" means a pension payable—

(a)   in respect of the services of the pensioner's deceased husband, or

(b)   by virtue of the pensioner's deceased husband having become entitled to a pension credit.'

40   Other pension schemes

(1) The Secretary of State may by regulations make provision for a pension to which subsection (2) applies to be increased, as a minimum, by reference to increases in the retail prices index, so far as not exceeding 5% per annum.

(2) This subsection applies to—

(a)   a pension provided to give effect to eligible pension credit rights of a member under a qualifying occupational pension scheme, and

(b)   a pension provided to give effect to safeguarded rights of a member under a personal pension scheme.

(3) In this section—

'eligible', in relation to pension credit rights, means of a description prescribed by regulations made by the Secretary of State;
'pension credit rights', in relation to an occupational pension scheme, means rights to future benefits under the scheme which are attributable (directly or indirectly) to a credit under section 29(1)(b) or under corresponding Northern Ireland legislation;

'qualifying occupational pension scheme' means an occupational pension scheme which is not a public service pension scheme;

'safeguarded rights' has the meaning given in section 68A of the Pension Schemes Act 1993.

Charges by pension arrangements

41   Charges in respect of pension sharing costs

(1) The Secretary of State may by regulations make provision for the purpose of enabling the person responsible for a pension arrangement involved in pension sharing to recover from the parties to pension sharing prescribed charges in respect of prescribed descriptions of pension sharing activity.

(2) Regulations under subsection (1) may include—

(a)   provision for the start of the implementation period for a pension credit to be postponed in prescribed circumstances;
(b)   provision, in relation to payments in respect of charges recoverable under the regulations, for reimbursement as between the parties to pension sharing;
(c)   provision, in relation to the recovery of charges by deduction from a pension credit, for the modification of Schedule 5;
(d)   provision for the recovery in prescribed circumstances of such additional amounts as may be determined in accordance with the regulations.

(3) For the purposes of regulations under subsection (1), the question of how much of a charge recoverable under the regulations is attributable to a party to pension sharing is to be determined as follows—

(a)   where the relevant order or provision includes provision about the apportionment of charges under this section, there is attributable to the party so much of the charge as is apportioned to him by that provision;
(b)   where the relevant order or provision does not include such provision, the charge is attributable to the transferor.

(4) For the purposes of subsection (1), a pension arrangement is involved in pension sharing if section 29 applies by virtue of an order or provision which relates to the arrangement.

(5) In that subsection, the reference to pension sharing activity is to activity attributable (directly or indirectly) to the involvement in pension sharing.

(6) In subsection (3)—

(a) the reference to the relevant order or provision is to the order or provision which gives rise to the pension sharing, and
(b) the reference to the transferor is to the person to whose rights that order or provision relates.

(7) In this section 'prescribed' means prescribed in regulations under subsection (1).

Adaptation of statutory schemes

42   Extension of scheme-making powers

(1) Power under an Act to establish a pension scheme shall include power to make provision for the provision, by reference to pension credits which derive from rights under—

(a) the scheme, or
(b) a scheme in relation to which the scheme is specified as an alternative for the purposes of paragraph 2 of Schedule 5,

of benefits to or in respect of those entitled to the credits.

(2) Subsection (1) is without prejudice to any other power.

(3) Subsection (1) shall apply in relation to Acts whenever passed.

(4) No obligation to consult shall apply in relation to the making, in exercise of a power under an Act to establish a pension scheme, of provision of a kind authorised by subsection (1).

(5) Any provision of, or under, an Act which makes benefits under a pension scheme established under an Act a charge on, or payable out of—

(a) the Consolidated Fund,
(b) the Scottish Consolidated Fund, or
(c) the Consolidated Fund of Northern Ireland,

shall be treated as including any benefits under the scheme which are attributable (directly or indirectly) to a pension credit which derives from rights to benefits charged on, or payable out of, that fund.

(6) In this section—

'pension credit' includes a credit under Northern Ireland legislation corresponding to section 29(1)(b);

'pension scheme' means a scheme or arrangement providing benefits, in the form of pensions or otherwise, payable on termination of service, or on death or retirement, to or in respect of persons to whom the scheme or arrangement applies.

43 Power to extend judicial pension schemes

(1) The appropriate minister may by regulations amend the Sheriffs' Pensions (Scotland) Act 1961, the Judicial Pensions Act 1981 or the Judicial Pensions and Retirement Act 1993 for the purpose of—

- (a) extending a pension scheme under the Act to include the provision, by reference to pension credits which derive from rights under—
  - (i) the scheme, or
  - (ii) a scheme in relation to which the scheme is specified as an alternative for the purposes of paragraph 2 of Schedule 5, of benefits to or in respect of those entitled to the credits, or
- (b) restricting the power of the appropriate minister to accept payments into a pension scheme under the Act, where the payments represent the cash equivalent of rights under another pension scheme which are attributable (directly or indirectly) to a pension credit.

(2) Regulations under subsection (1)—

- (a) may make benefits provided by virtue of paragraph (a) of that subsection a charge on, and payable out of, the Consolidated Fund;
- (b) may confer power to make subordinate legislation, including subordinate legislation which provides for calculation of the value of rights in accordance with guidance from time to time prepared by a person specified in the subordinate legislation.

(3) The appropriate minister for the purposes of subsection (1) is—

- (a) in relation to a pension scheme whose ordinary members are limited to those who hold judicial office whose jurisdiction is exercised exclusively in relation to Scotland, the Secretary of State, and
- (b) in relation to any other pension scheme, the Lord Chancellor.

(4) In this section—

'pension credit' includes a credit under Northern Ireland legislation corresponding to section 29(1)(b);

'pension scheme' means a scheme or arrangement providing benefits, in the form of pensions or otherwise, payable on termination of service, or on death or retirement, to or in respect of persons to whom the scheme or arrangement applies.

Supplementary

44 Disapplication of restrictions on alienation

(1) Nothing in any of the following provisions (restrictions on alienation of pension rights) applies in relation to any order or provision falling within section 28(1)—

    (a) section 203(1) and (2) of the Army Act 1955, section 203(1) and (2) of the Air Force Act 1955, section 128G(1) and (2) of the Naval Discipline Act 1957 and section 159(4) and (4A) of the Pension Schemes Act 1993,

    (b) section 91 of the Pensions Act 1995,

    (c) any provision of any enactment (whether passed or made before or after this Act is passed) corresponding to any of the enactments mentioned in paragraphs (a) and (b), and

    (d) any provision of a pension arrangement corresponding to any of those enactments.

(2) In this section, 'enactment' includes an enactment comprised in subordinate legislation (within the meaning of the Interpretation Act 1978).

45 Information

(1) The Secretary of State may by regulations require the person responsible for a pension arrangement involved in pension sharing to supply to such persons as he may specify in the regulations such information relating to anything which follows from the application of section 29 as he may so specify.

(2) Section 168 of the Pension Schemes Act 1993 (breach of regulations) shall apply as if this section were contained in that Act (otherwise than in Chapter II of Part VII).

(3) For the purposes of this section, a pension arrangement is involved in pension sharing if section 29 applies by virtue of an order or provision which relates to the arrangement.

46 Interpretation of Chapter I

(1) In this Chapter—

'implementation period', in relation to a pension credit, has the meaning given by section 34;

'occupational pension scheme' has the meaning given by section 1 of the Pension Schemes Act 1993;

'pension arrangement' means—

(a)   an occupational pension scheme,

(b)   a personal pension scheme,

(c)   a retirement annuity contract,

(d)   an annuity or insurance policy purchased, or transferred, for the purpose of giving effect to rights under an occupational pension scheme or a personal pension scheme, and

(e)   an annuity purchased, or entered into, for the purpose of discharging liability in respect of a credit under section 29(1)(b) or under corresponding Northern Ireland legislation;

'pension credit' means a credit under section 29(1)(b);

'pension debit' means a debit under section 29(1)(a);

'pensionable service', in relation to a member of an occupational pension scheme, means service in any description or category of employment to which the scheme relates which qualifies the member (on the assumption that it continues for the appropriate period) for pension or other benefits under the scheme;

'personal pension scheme' has the meaning given by section 1 of the Pension Schemes Act 1993;

'retirement annuity contract' means a contract or scheme approved under Chapter III of Part XIV of the Income and Corporation Taxes Act 1988;

'shareable rights' has the meaning given by section 27(2);

'trustees or managers', in relation to an occupational pension scheme or a personal pension scheme means—

(a)   in the case of a scheme established under a trust, the trustees of the scheme, and

(b)   in any other case, the managers of the scheme.

(2) In this Chapter, references to the person responsible for a pension arrangement are—

(a)   in the case of an occupational pension scheme or a personal pension scheme, to the trustees or managers of the scheme,

(b) in the case of a retirement annuity contract or an annuity falling within paragraph (d) or (e) of the definition of 'pension arrangement' in subsection (1), to the provider of the annuity, and

(c) in the case of an insurance policy falling within paragraph (d) of the definition of that expression, to the insurer.

(3) In determining what is 'pensionable service' for the purposes of this Chapter—

(a) service notionally attributable for any purpose of the scheme is to be disregarded, and

(b) no account is to be taken of any rules of the scheme by which a period of service can be treated for any purpose as being longer or shorter than it actually is.

CHAPTER II

SHARING OF STATE SCHEME RIGHTS

47 Shareable state scheme rights

(1) Pension sharing is available under this Chapter in relation to a person's shareable state scheme rights.

(2) For the purposes of this Chapter, a person's shareable state scheme rights are—

(a) his entitlement, or prospective entitlement, to a Category A retirement pension by virtue of section 44(3)(b) of the Contributions and Benefits Act (earnings-related additional pension), and

(b) his entitlement, or prospective entitlement, to a pension under section 55A of that Act (shared additional pension).

48 Activation of benefit sharing

(1) Section 49 applies on the taking effect of any of the following relating to a person's shareable state scheme rights—

(a) a pension sharing order under the Matrimonial Causes Act 1973,

(b) provision which corresponds to the provision which may be made by such an order and which—

(i) is contained in a qualifying agreement between the parties to a marriage, and

(ii) takes effect on the dissolution of the marriage under the Family Law Act 1996,

(c) provision which corresponds to the provision which may be made by such an order and which—
- (i) is contained in a qualifying agreement between the parties to a marriage or former marriage, and
- (ii) takes effect after the dissolution of the marriage under the Family Law Act 1996,

(d) an order under Part III of the Matrimonial and Family Proceedings Act 1984 (financial relief in England and Wales in relation to overseas divorce etc.) corresponding to such an order as is mentioned in paragraph (a),

(e) a pension sharing order under the Family Law (Scotland) Act 1985,

(f) provision which corresponds to the provision which may be made by such an order and which—
- (i) is contained in a qualifying agreement between the parties to a marriage,
- (ii) is in such form as the Secretary of State may prescribe by regulations, and
- (iii) takes effect on the grant, in relation to the marriage, of decree of divorce under the Divorce (Scotland) Act 1976 or of declarator of nullity,

(g) an order under Part IV of the Matrimonial and Family Proceedings Act 1984 (financial relief in Scotland in relation to overseas divorce etc.) corresponding to such an order as is mentioned in paragraph (e),

(h) a pension sharing order under Northern Ireland legislation, and

(i) an order under Part IV of the Matrimonial and Family Proceedings (Northern Ireland) Order 1989 (financial relief in Northern Ireland in relation to overseas divorce etc.) corresponding to such an order as is mentioned in paragraph (h).

(2) For the purposes of subsection (1)(b) and (c), a qualifying agreement is one which—

(a) has been entered into in such circumstances as the Lord Chancellor may prescribe by regulations, and

(b) satisfies such requirements as the Lord Chancellor may so prescribe.

(3) For the purposes of subsection (1)(f), a qualifying agreement is one which—

(a) has been entered into in such circumstances as the Secretary of State may prescribe by regulations, and

(b)   is registered in the Books of Council and Session.

(4) Subsection (1)(b) does not apply if the provision relates to rights which are the subject of a pension sharing order under the Matrimonial Causes Act 1973 in relation to the marriage.

(5) Subsection (1)(c) does not apply if—

(a)   the marriage was dissolved by an order under section 3 of the Family Law Act 1996 (divorce not preceded by separation) and the satisfaction of the requirements of section 9(2) of that Act (settlement of future financial arrangements) was a precondition to the making of the order,

(b)   the provision relates to rights which are the subject of a pension sharing order under the Matrimonial Causes Act 1973 in relation to the marriage, or

(c)   shareable state scheme rights have already been the subject of pension sharing between the parties.

(6) For the purposes of this section, an order or provision falling within subsection (1)(e), (f) or (g) shall be deemed never to have taken effect if the Secretary of State does not receive before the end of the period of 2 months beginning with the relevant date—

(a)   copies of the relevant matrimonial documents, and

(b)   such information relating to the transferor and transferee as the Secretary of State may prescribe by regulations under section 34(1)(b)(ii).

(7) The relevant date for the purposes of subsection (6) is—

(a)   in the case of an order or provision falling within subsection (1)(e) or (f), the date of the extract of the decree or declarator responsible for the divorce or annulment to which the order or provision relates, and

(b)   in the case of an order falling within subsection (1)(g), the date of disposal of the application under section 28 of the Matrimonial and Family Proceedings Act 1984.

(8) The reference in subsection (6)(a) to the relevant matrimonial documents is—

(a)   in the case of an order falling within subsection (1)(e) or (g), to copies of the order and the order, decree or declarator responsible for the divorce or annulment to which it relates, and

(b)   in the case of provision falling within subsection (1)(f), to—

    (i)   copies of the provision and the order, decree or declarator responsible for the divorce or annulment to which it relates, and

    (ii)   documentary evidence that the agreement containing the provision is one to which subsection (3)(a) applies.

(9) The sheriff may, on the application of any person having an interest, make an order—

(a)   extending the period of 2 months referred to in subsection (6), and

(b)   if that period has already expired, providing that, if the Secretary of State receives the documents and information concerned before the end of the period specified in the order, subsection (6) is to be treated as never having applied.

49   Creation of state scheme pension debits and credits

(1) On the application of this section—

(a)   the transferor becomes subject, for the purposes of Part II of the Contributions and Benefits Act (contributory benefits), to a debit of the appropriate amount, and

(b)   the transferee becomes entitled, for those purposes, to a credit of that amount.

(2) Where the relevant order or provision specifies a percentage value to be transferred, the appropriate amount for the purposes of subsection (1) is the specified percentage of the cash equivalent on the transfer day of the transferor's shareable state scheme rights immediately before that day.

(3) Where the relevant order or provision specifies an amount to be transferred, the appropriate amount for the purposes of subsection (1) is the lesser of—

(a)   the specified amount, and

(b)   the cash equivalent on the transfer day of the transferor's relevant state scheme rights immediately before that day.

(4) Cash equivalents for the purposes of this section shall be calculated in accordance with regulations made by the Secretary of State.

(5) In determining prospective entitlement to a Category A retirement pension for the purposes of this section, only tax years before that in which the transfer day falls shall be taken into account.

(6) In this section—

'relevant order or provision' means the order or provision by virtue of which this section applies;

'transfer day' means the day on which the relevant order or provision takes effect;

'transferor' means the person to whose rights the relevant order or provision relates;

'transferee' means the person for whose benefit the relevant order or provision is made.

50   Effect of state scheme pension debits and credits

(1) Schedule 6 (which amends the Contributions and Benefits Act for the purpose of giving effect to debits and credits under section 49(1)) shall have effect.

(2) Section 55C of that Act (which is inserted by that Schedule) shall have effect, in relation to incremental periods (within the meaning of that section) beginning on or after 6th April 2010, with the following amendments—

   (a)   in subsection (3), for 'period of enhancement' there is substituted 'period of deferment',
   (b)   in subsection (4), for '1/7th per cent.' there is substituted '1/5th per cent.',
   (c)   in subsection (7), for 'period of enhancement', in both places, there is substituted 'period of deferment', and
   (d)   in subsection (9), the definition of 'period of enhancement' (and the preceding 'and') are omitted.

51   Interpretation of Chapter II

In this Chapter—

'shareable state scheme rights' has the meaning given by section 47(2); and 'tax year' has the meaning given by section 122(1) of the Contributions and Benefits Act.

. . .

SCHEDULE 3   Section 19

PENSION SHARING ORDERS: ENGLAND AND WALES

1. The Matrimonial Causes Act 1973 is amended as follows.

2. After section 21 there is inserted—

'21A   Pension sharing orders

(1) For the purposes of this Act, a pension sharing order is an order which—

- (a) provides that one party's—
  - (i) shareable rights under a specified pension arrangement, or
  - (ii) shareable state scheme rights,
  be subject to pension sharing for the benefit of the other party, and
- (b) specifies the percentage value to be transferred.

(2) In subsection (1) above—

- (a) the reference to shareable rights under a pension arrangement is to rights in relation to which pension sharing is available under Chapter I of Part IV of the Welfare Reform and Pensions Act 1999, or under corresponding Northern Ireland legislation.
- (b) the reference to shareable state scheme rights is to rights in relation to which pension sharing is available under Chapter II of Part IV of the Welfare Reform and Pensions Act 1999, or under corresponding Northern Ireland legislation, and
- (c) "party" means a party to a marriage.'

3. In section 24 (property adjustment orders in connection with divorce proceedings, etc.), in paragraphs (c) and (d) of subsection (1), there is inserted at the end ', other than one in the form of a pension arrangement (within the meaning of section 25D below'.

4. After section 24A there is inserted—

'24B   Pension sharing orders in connection with divorce proceedings etc.

(1) On granting a decree of divorce or a decree of nullity of marriage or at any time thereafter (whether before or after the decree is made

absolute), the court may, on an application made under this section, make one or more pension sharing orders in relation to the marriage.

(2) A pension sharing order under this section is not to take effect unless the decree on or after which it is made has been made absolute.

(3) A pension sharing order under this section may not be made in relation to a pension arrangement which—

    (a) is the subject of a pension sharing order in relation to the marriage, or

    (b) has been the subject of pension sharing between the parties to the marriage.

(4) A pension sharing order under this section may not be made in relation to shareable state scheme rights if—

    (a) such rights are the subject of a pension sharing order in relation to the marriage, or

    (b) such rights have been the subject of pension sharing between the parties to the marriage.

(5) A pension sharing order under this section may not be made in relation to the rights of a person under a pension arrangement if there is in force a requirement imposed by virtue of section 25B or 25C below which relates to benefits or future benefits to which he is entitled under the pension arrangement.

24C Pension sharing orders: duty to stay

(1) No pension sharing order may be made so as to take effect before the end of such period after the making of the order as may be prescribed by regulations made by the Lord Chancellor.

(2) The power to make regulations under this section shall be exercisable by statutory instrument which shall be subject to annulment in pursuance of a resolution of either House of Parliament.

24D Pension sharing orders: apportionment of charges

If a pension sharing order relates to rights under a pension arrangement, the court may include in the order provision about the apportionment between the parties of any charge under section 41 of the Welfare Reform and Pensions Act 1999 (charges in respect of pension sharing costs), or under corresponding Northern Ireland legislation.'

5. In section 25 (matters to which the court is to have regard in deciding how to exercise its powers with respect to financial relief)—

    (a)   in subsection (1), for 'or 24A' there is substituted ', 24A or 24B', and

    (b)   in subsection (2), for 'or 24A' there is substituted ', 24A or 24B'.

6. In section 25A(1) (court's duty to consider desirability of exercising power to achieve clean break), for 'or 24A' there is substituted ', 24A or 24B'.

7.—(1) Section 31 (variation, discharge etc. of certain orders for financial relief) is amended as follows.

(2) In subsection (2), at the end there is inserted—

    '(g)   a pension sharing order under section 24B above which is made at a time before the decree has been made absolute.'

(3) After subsection (4) there is inserted—

'(4A) In relation to an order which falls within paragraph (g) of subsection (2) above ("the subsection (2) order")—

    (a)   the powers conferred by this section may be exercised—

        (i)   only on an application made before the subsection (2) order has or, but for paragraph (b) below, would have taken effect; and

        (ii)   only if, at the time when the application is made, the decree has not been made absolute; and

    (b)   an application made in accordance with paragraph (a) above prevents the subsection (2) order from taking effect before the application has been dealt with.

(4B) No variation of a pension sharing order shall be made so as to take effect before the decree is made absolute.

(4C) The variation of a pension sharing order prevents the order taking effect before the end of such period after the making of the variation as may be prescribed by regulations made by the Lord Chancellor.'

(4) In subsection (5)—

    (a)   for '(7F)' there is substituted '(7G)',

    (b)   for 'or (e)' there is substituted ', (e) or (g)', and

    (c)   after 'property adjustment order' there is inserted 'or pension sharing order'.

(5) In subsection (7B), after paragraph (b) there is inserted—

'(ba) one or more pension sharing orders;'.

(6) After subsection (7F) there is inserted—

'(7G) Subsections (3) to (5) of section 24B above apply in relation to a pension sharing order under subsection (7B) above as they apply in relation to a pension sharing order under that section.'

(7) After subsection (14) there is inserted—

'(15) The power to make regulations under subsection (4C) above shall be exercisable by statutory instrument which shall be subject to annulment in pursuance of a resolution of either House of Parliament.'

8. In section 33A (consent orders), in subsection (3), in the definition of 'order for financial relief', after '24A' there is inserted ', 24B'.

9. In section 37 (avoidance of transactions intended to prevent or reduce financial relief), in subsection (1), after '24,' there is inserted '24B,'.

10. After section 40 there is inserted—

'40A   Appeals relating to pension sharing orders which have taken effect

(1) Subsections (2) and (3) below apply where an appeal against a pension sharing order is begun on or after the day on which the order takes effect.

(2) If the pension sharing order relates to a person's rights under a pension arrangement, the appeal court may not set aside or vary the order if the person responsible for the pension arrangement has acted to his detriment in reliance on the taking effect of the order.

(3) If the pension sharing order relates to a person's shareable state scheme rights, the appeal court may not set aside or vary the order if the Secretary of State has acted to his detriment in reliance on the taking effect of the order.

(4) In determining for the purposes of subsection (2) or (3) above whether a person has acted to his detriment in reliance on the taking effect of the order, the appeal court may disregard any detriment which in its opinion is insignificant.

(5) Where subsection (2) or (3) above applies, the appeal court may make such further orders (including one or more pension sharing

orders) as it thinks fit for the purpose of putting the parties in the position it considers appropriate.

(6) Section 24C above only applies to a pension sharing order under this section if the decision of the appeal court can itself be the subject of an appeal.

(7) In subsection (2) above, the reference to the person responsible for the pension arrangement is to be read in accordance with section 25D(4) above.'

11. In section 52 (interpretation), in subsection (2), for 'and' at the end of paragraph (a) there is substituted—

'(aa) references to pension sharing orders shall be construed in accordance with section 21A above; and'.

SCHEDULE 4   Section 21

AMENDMENTS OF SECTIONS 25B TO 25D OF THE MATRIMONIAL CAUSES ACT 1973

1.—(1) Section 25B of the Matrimonial Causes Act 1973 is amended as follows.

(2) In subsection (1), for 'scheme', wherever occurring, there is substituted 'arrangement'.

(3) Subsection (2) ceases to have effect.

(4) In subsection (3), for 'scheme' there is substituted 'arrangement'.

(5) In subsection (4)—

   (a) for 'scheme', wherever occurring, there is substituted 'arrangement', and
   (b) for 'trustees or managers of' there is substituted 'person responsible for'.

(6) For subsection (5) there is substituted—

   '(5) The order must express the amount of any payment required to be made by virtue of subsection (4) above as a percentage of the payment which becomes due to the party with pension rights.'

(7) In subsection (6)—

(a) for 'trustees or managers', in the first place, there is substituted 'person responsible for the arrangement', and

(b) for 'the trustees or managers', in the second place, there is substituted 'his'.

(8) In subsection (7)—

(a) for the words from 'may require any' to 'those benefits' there is substituted 'has a right of commutation under the arrangement, the order may require him to exercise it to any extent',

(b) for 'the payment of any amount commuted' there is substituted 'any payment due in consequence of commutation', and

(c) for 'scheme' there is substituted 'arrangement'.

(9) After that subsection there is inserted—

'(7A) The power conferred by subsection (7) above may not be exercised for the purpose of commuting a benefit payable to the party with pension rights to a benefit payable to the other party.

(7B) The power conferred by subsection (4) or (7) above may not be exercised in relation to a pension arrangement which—

(a) is the subject of a pension sharing order in relation to the marriage, or

(b) has been the subject of pension sharing between the parties to the marriage.

(7C) In subsection (1) above, references to benefits under a pension arrangement include any benefits by way of pension, whether under a pension arrangement or not.'

2.—(1) Section 25C of that Act is amended as follows.

(2) In subsection (1), for 'scheme' there is substituted 'arrangement'.

(3) In subsection (2)—

(a) in paragraph (a)—

(i) for the words from 'trustees' to 'have' there is substituted 'person responsible for the pension arrangement in question has', and

(ii) for 'them' there is substituted 'him', and

(b) in paragraph (c), for 'trustees or managers of the pension scheme' there is substituted 'person responsible for the pension arrangement'.

(4) In subsection (3)—

  (a) for 'trustees or managers' there is substituted 'person responsible for the arrangement', and

  (b) for 'the trustees, or managers,' there is substituted 'his'.

(5) At the end there is inserted—

    '(4) The powers conferred by this section may not be exercised in relation to a pension arrangement which—

    (a) is the subject of a pension sharing order in relation to the marriage, or

    (b) has been the subject of pension sharing between the parties to the marriage.'

3.—(1) Section 25D of that Act is amended as follows.

(2) For subsection (1) there is substituted—

    '(1) Where—

    (a) an order made under section 23 above by virtue of section 25B or 25C above imposes any requirement on the person responsible for a pension arrangement ("the first arrangement") and the party with pension rights acquires rights under another pension arrangement ("the new arrangement") which are derived (directly or indirectly) from the whole of his rights under the first arrangement, and

    (b) the person responsible for the new arrangement has been given notice in accordance with regulations made by the Lord Chancellor,

    the order shall have effect as if it had been made instead in respect of the person responsible for the new arrangement.'

(3) In subsection (2)—

  (a) for 'Regulations may' there is substituted 'The Lord Chancellor may by regulations',

  (b) in paragraph (a), for 'trustees or managers of a pension scheme' there is substituted 'person responsible for a pension arrangement',

  (c) after the paragraph there is inserted—

    '(ab) make, in relation to payment under a mistaken belief as to the continuation in force of a provision included by virtue of section 25B or 25C above in an order under section 23 above, provision about the rights or liabilities of the payer, the payee or the person to whom the payment was due,'

(d) after paragraph (b) there is inserted—

'(ba) make provision for the person responsible for a pension arrangement to be discharged in prescribed circumstances from a requirement imposed by virtue of section 25B or 25C above,'

(e) paragraphs (c) and (d) are omitted,
(f) for paragraph (e) there is substituted—

'(e) make provision about calculation and verification in relation to the valuation of—
(i) benefits under a pension arrangement, or
(ii) shareable state scheme rights,
for the purposes of the court's functions in connection with the exercise of any of its powers under this Part of this Act.', and

(g) the words after paragraph (e) are omitted.

(4) After that subsection there is inserted—

'(2A) Regulations under subsection (2)(e) above may include—

(a) provision for calculation or verification in accordance with guidance from time to time prepared by a prescribed person, and
(b) provision by reference to regulations under section 30 or 49(4) of the Welfare Reform and Pensions Act 1999.

(2B) Regulations under subsection (2) above may make different provision for different cases.

(2C) Power to make regulations under this section shall be exercisable by statutory instrument which shall be subject to annulment in pursuance of a resolution of either House of Parliament.'

(5) For subsections (3) and (4) there is substituted—

'(3) In this section and sections 25B and 25C above—

"occupational pension scheme" has the same meaning as in the Pension Schemes Act 1993;

"the party with pension rights" means the party to the marriage who has or is likely to have benefits under a pension arrangement and "the other party" means the other party to the marriage;

"pension arrangement" means—

(a) an occupational pension scheme,

(b) a personal pension scheme,

(c) a retirement annuity contract,

(d) an annuity or insurance policy purchased, or transferred, for the purpose of giving effect to rights under an occupational pension scheme or a personal pension scheme, and

(e) an annuity purchased, or entered into, for the purpose of discharging liability in respect of a pension credit under section 29(1)(b) of the Welfare Reform and Pensions Act 1999 or under corresponding Northern Ireland legislation;

"personal pension scheme" has the same meaning as in the Pension Schemes Act 1993;

"prescribed" means prescribed by regulations;

"retirement annuity contract" means a contract or scheme approved under Chapter III of Part XIV of the Income and Corporation Taxes Act 1988;

"shareable state scheme rights" has the same meaning as in section 21A(1) above; and

"trustees or managers", in relation to an occupational pension scheme or a personal pension scheme, means—

(a) in the case of a scheme established under a trust, the trustees of the scheme, and

(b) in any other case, the managers of the scheme.

(4) In this section and sections 25B and 25C above, references to the person responsible for a pension arrangement are—

(a) in the case of an occupational pension scheme or a personal pension scheme, to the trustees or managers of the scheme,

(b) in the case of a retirement annuity contract or an annuity falling within paragraph (d) or (e) of the definition of "pension arrangement" above, the provider of the annuity, and

(c) in the case of an insurance policy falling within paragraph (d) of the definition of that expression, the insurer.'

SCHEDULE 5   Section 35

PENSION CREDITS: MODE OF DISCHARGE

Funded pension schemes

1.—(1) This paragraph applies to a pension credit which derives from—

(a)   a funded occupational pension scheme, or
(b)   a personal pension scheme.

(2) The trustees or managers of the scheme from which a pension credit to which this paragraph applies derives may discharge their liability in respect of the credit by conferring appropriate rights under that scheme on the person entitled to the credit—

(a)   with his consent, or
(b)   in accordance with regulations made by the Secretary of State.

(3) The trustees or managers of the scheme from which a pension credit to which this paragraph applies derives may discharge their liability in respect of the credit by paying the amount of the credit to the person responsible for a qualifying arrangement with a view to acquiring rights under that arrangement for the person entitled to the credit if—

(a)   the qualifying arrangement is not disqualified as a destination for the credit,
(b)   the person responsible for that arrangement is able and willing to accept payment in respect of the credit, and
(c)   payment is made with the consent of the person entitled to the credit, or in accordance with regulations made by the Secretary of State.

(4) For the purposes of sub-paragraph (2), no account is to be taken of consent of the person entitled to the pension credit unless—

(a)   it is given after receipt of notice in writing of an offer to discharge liability in respect of the credit by making a payment under subparagraph (3), or
(b)   it is not withdrawn within 7 days of receipt of such notice.

Unfunded public service pension schemes

2.—(1) This paragraph applies to a pension credit which derives from an occupational pension scheme which is—

(a) not funded, and

(b) a public service pension scheme.

(2) The trustees or managers of the scheme from which a pension credit to which this paragraph applies derives may discharge their liability in respect of the credit by conferring appropriate rights under that scheme on the person entitled to the credit.

(3) If such a scheme as is mentioned in sub-paragraph (1) is closed to new members, the appropriate authority in relation to that scheme may by regulations specify another public service pension scheme as an alternative to it for the purposes of this paragraph.

(4) Where the trustees or managers of a scheme in relation to which an alternative is specified under sub-paragraph (3) are subject to liability in respect of a pension credit, they may—

(a) discharge their liability in respect of the credit by securing that appropriate rights are conferred on the person entitled to the credit by the trustees or managers of the alternative scheme, and

(b) for the purpose of so discharging their liability, require the trustees or managers of the alternative scheme to take such steps as may be required.

(5) In sub-paragraph (3), 'the appropriate authority', in relation to a public service pension scheme, means such Minister of the Crown or government department as may be designated by the Treasury as having responsibility for the scheme.

Other unfunded occupational pension schemes

3.—(1) This paragraph applies to a pension credit which derives from an occupational pension scheme which is—

(a) not funded, and

(b) not a public service pension scheme.

(2) The trustees or managers of the scheme from which a pension credit to which this paragraph applies derives may discharge their liability in respect of the credit by conferring appropriate rights under that scheme on the person entitled to the credit.

(3) The trustees or managers of the scheme from which a pension credit to which this paragraph applies derives may discharge their liability in respect

of the credit by paying the amount of the credit to the person responsible for a qualifying arrangement with a view to acquiring rights under that arrangement for the person entitled to the credit if—

    (a)   the qualifying arrangement is not disqualified as a destination for the credit,

    (b)   the person responsible for that arrangement is able and willing to accept payment in respect of the credit, and

    (c)   payment is made with the consent of the person entitled to the credit, or in accordance with regulations made by the Secretary of State.

Other pension arrangements

4.—(1) This paragraph applies to a pension credit which derives from—

    (a)   a retirement annuity contract,

    (b)   an annuity or insurance policy purchased or transferred for the purpose of giving effect to rights under an occupational pension scheme or a personal pension scheme, or

    (c)   an annuity purchased, or entered into, for the purpose of discharging liability in respect of a pension credit.

(2) The person responsible for the pension arrangement from which a pension credit to which this paragraph applies derives may discharge his liability in respect of the credit by paying the amount of the credit to the person responsible for a qualifying arrangement with a view to acquiring rights under that arrangement for the person entitled to the credit if—

    (a)   the qualifying arrangement is not disqualified as a destination for the credit,

    (b)   the person responsible for that arrangement is able and willing to accept payment in respect of the credit, and

    (c)   payment is made with the consent of the person entitled to the credit, or in accordance with regulations made by the Secretary of State.

(3) The person responsible for the pension arrangement from which a pension credit to which this paragraph applies derives may discharge his liability in respect of the credit by entering into an annuity contract with the person entitled to the credit if the contract is not disqualified as a destination for the credit.

(4) The person responsible for the pension arrangement from which a pension credit to which this paragraph applies derives may, in such

circumstances as the Secretary of State may prescribe by regulations, discharge his liability in respect of the credit by assuming an obligation to provide an annuity for the person entitled to the credit.

(5) In sub-paragraph (1)(c), 'pension credit' includes a credit under Northern Ireland legislation corresponding to section 29(1)(b).

Appropriate rights

5. For the purposes of this Schedule, rights conferred on the person entitled to a pension credit are appropriate if—

   (a)   they are conferred with effect from, and including, the day on which the order, or provision, under which the credit arises takes effect, and
   (b)   their value, when calculated in accordance with regulations made by the Secretary of State, equals the amount of the credit.

Qualifying arrangements

6.—(1) The following are qualifying arrangements for the purposes of this Schedule—

   (a)   an occupational pension scheme,
   (b)   a personal pension scheme,
   (c)   an appropriate annuity contract,
   (d)   an appropriate policy of insurance, and
   (e)   an overseas arrangement within the meaning of the Contracting-out (Transfer and Transfer Payment) Regulations 1996.

(2) An annuity contract or policy of insurance is appropriate for the purposes of sub-paragraph (1) if, at the time it is entered into or taken out, the insurance company with which it is entered into or taken out—

   (a)   is carrying on ordinary long-term insurance business in the United Kingdom or any other member State, and
   (b)   satisfies such requirements as the Secretary of State may prescribe by regulations.

(3) In this paragraph, 'ordinary long-term insurance business' has the same meaning as in the Insurance Companies Act 1982.

Disqualification as destination for pension credit

7.—(1) If a pension credit derives from a pension arrangement which is approved for the purposes of Part XIV of the Income and Corporation Taxes Act 1988, an arrangement is disqualified as a destination for the credit unless—

(a)   it is also approved for those purposes, or
(b)   it satisfies such requirements as the Secretary of State may prescribe by regulations.

(2) If the rights by reference to which the amount of a pension credit is determined are or include contracted-out rights or safeguarded rights, an arrangement is disqualified as a destination for the credit unless—

(a)   it is of a description prescribed by the Secretary of State by regulations, and
(b)   it satisfies such requirements as he may so prescribe.

(3) An occupational pension scheme is disqualified as a destination for a pension credit unless the rights to be acquired under the arrangement by the person entitled to the credit are rights whose value, when calculated in accordance with regulations made by the Secretary of State, equals the credit.

(4) An annuity contract or insurance policy is disqualified as a destination for a pension credit in such circumstances as the Secretary of State may prescribe by regulations.

(5) The requirements which may be prescribed under sub-paragraph (1)(b) include, in particular, requirements of the Inland Revenue.

(6) In sub-paragraph (2)—

'contracted-out rights' means such rights under, or derived from—

(a)   an occupational pension scheme contracted-out by virtue of section 9(2) or (3) of the Pension Schemes Act 1993, or
(b)   a personal pension scheme which is an appropriate scheme for the purposes of that Act,

as the Secretary of State may prescribe by regulations;

'safeguarded rights' has the meaning given by section 68A of the Pension Schemes Act 1993.

Adjustments to amount of pension credit

8.—(1) If—

    (a) a pension credit derives from an occupational pension scheme,

    (b) the scheme is one to which section 56 of the Pensions Act 1995 (minimum funding requirement for funded salary related schemes) applies,

    (c) the scheme is underfunded on the valuation day, and

    (d) such circumstances as the Secretary of State may prescribe by regulations apply,

paragraph 1(3) shall have effect in relation to the credit as if the reference to the amount of the credit were to such lesser amount as may be determined in accordance with regulations made by the Secretary of State.

(2) Whether a scheme is underfunded for the purposes of sub-paragraph (1)(c) shall be determined in accordance with regulations made by the Secretary of State.

(3) For the purposes of that provision, the valuation day is the day by reference to which the cash equivalent on which the amount of the pension credit depends falls to be calculated.

9. If—

    (a) a person's shareable rights under a pension arrangement have become subject to a pension debit, and

    (b) the person responsible for the arrangement makes a payment which is referable to those rights without knowing of the pension debit,

this Schedule shall have effect as if the amount of the corresponding pension credit were such lesser amount as may be determined in accordance with regulations made by the Secretary of State.

10. The Secretary of State may by regulations make provision for paragraph 1(3), 3(3) or 4(2) to have effect, where payment is made after the end of the implementation period for the pension credit, as if the reference to the amount of the credit were to such larger amount as may be determined in accordance with the regulations.

General

11. Liability in respect of a pension credit shall be treated as discharged if the effect of paragraph 8(1) or 9 is to reduce it to zero.

12. Liability in respect of a pension credit may not be discharged otherwise than in accordance with this Schedule.

13. Regulations under paragraph 5(b) or 7(3) may provide for calculation of the value of rights in accordance with guidance from time to time prepared by a person specified in the regulations.

14. In this Schedule—

'funded', in relation to an occupational pension scheme, means that the scheme meets its liabilities out of a fund accumulated for the purpose during the life of the scheme;

'public service pension scheme' has the same meaning as in the Pension Schemes Act 1993.

SCHEDULE 6   Section 50

EFFECT OF STATE SCHEME PENSION DEBITS AND CREDITS

1. The Contributions and Benefits Act is amended as follows.

2. After section 45A there is inserted—

'45B   Reduction of additional pension in Category A retirement pension: pension sharing

(1) The weekly rate of the additional pension in a Category A retirement pension shall be reduced as follows in any case where—

    (a)   the pensioner has become subject to a state scheme pension debit, and

    (b)   the debit is to any extent referable to the additional pension.

(2) If the pensioner became subject to the debit in or after the final relevant year, the weekly rate of the additional pension shall be reduced by the appropriate weekly amount.

(3) If the pensioner became subject to the debit before the final relevant year, the weekly rate of the additional pension shall be reduced by the appropriate weekly amount multiplied by the relevant revaluation percentage.

(4) The appropriate weekly amount for the purposes of subsections (2) and (3) above is the weekly rate, expressed in terms of the valuation day, at which the cash equivalent, on that day, of the pension

mentioned in subsection (5) below is equal to so much of the debit as is referable to the additional pension.

(5) The pension referred to above is a notional pension for the pensioner by virtue of section 44(3)(b) above which becomes payable on the later of—

(a)   his attaining pensionable age, and
(b)   the valuation day.

(6) For the purposes of subsection (3) above, the relevant revaluation percentage is the percentage specified, in relation to earnings factors for the tax year in which the pensioner became subject to the debit, by the last order under section 148 of the Administration Act to come into force before the end of the final relevant year.

(7) Cash equivalents for the purposes of this section shall be calculated in accordance with regulations.

(8) In this section—

"final relevant year" means the tax year immediately preceding that in which the pensioner attains pensionable age;

"state scheme pension debit" means a debit under section 49(1)(a) of the Welfare Reform and Pensions Act 1999 (debit for the purposes of this Part of this Act);

"valuation day" means the day on which the pensioner became subject to the state scheme pension debit.'

3. After section 55 there is inserted—

'Shared additional pension

55A   Shared additional pension

(1) A person shall be entitled to a shared additional pension if he is—

(a)   over pensionable age, and
(b)   entitled to a state scheme pension credit.

(2) A person's entitlement to a shared additional pension shall continue throughout his life.

(3) The weekly rate of a shared additional pension shall be the appropriate weekly amount, unless the pensioner's entitlement to the

state scheme pension credit arose before the final relevant year, in which case it shall be that amount multiplied by the relevant revaluation percentage.

(4) The appropriate weekly amount for the purposes of subsection (3) above is the weekly rate, expressed in terms of the valuation day, at which the cash equivalent, on that day, of the pensioner's entitlement, or prospective entitlement, to the shared additional pension is equal to the state scheme pension credit.

(5) The relevant revaluation percentage for the purposes of that subsection is the percentage specified, in relation to earnings factors for the tax year in which the entitlement to the state scheme pension credit arose, by the last order under section 148 of the Administration Act to come into force before the end of the final relevant year.

(6) Cash equivalents for the purposes of this section shall be calculated in accordance with regulations.

(7) In this section—

"final relevant year" means the tax year immediately preceding that in which the pensioner attains pensionable age;

"state scheme pension credit" means a credit under section 49(1)(b) of the Welfare Reform and Pensions Act 1999 (credit for the purposes of this Part of this Act);

"valuation day" means the day on which the pensioner becomes entitled to the state scheme pension credit.

55B Reduction of shared additional pension: pension sharing

(1) The weekly rate of a shared additional pension shall be reduced as follows in any case where—

    (a) the pensioner has become subject to a state scheme pension debit, and
    (b) the debit is to any extent referable to the pension.

(2) If the pensioner became subject to the debit in or after the final relevant year, the weekly rate of the pension shall be reduced by the appropriate weekly amount.

(3) If the pensioner became subject to the debit before the final relevant year, the weekly rate of the additional pension shall be reduced

by the appropriate weekly amount multiplied by the relevant revaluation percentage.

(4) The appropriate weekly amount for the purposes of subsections (2) and (3) above is the weekly rate, expressed in terms of the valuation day, at which the cash equivalent, on that day, of the pension mentioned in subsection (5) below is equal to so much of the debit as is referable to the shared additional pension.

(5) The pension referred to above is a notional pension for the pensioner by virtue of section 55A above which becomes payable on the later of—

(a)   his attaining pensionable age, and
(b)   the valuation day.

(6) For the purposes of subsection (3) above, the relevant revaluation percentage is the percentage specified, in relation to earnings factors for the tax year in which the pensioner became subject to the debit, by the last order under section 148 of the Administration Act to come into force before the end of the final relevant year.

(7) Cash equivalents for the purposes of this section shall be calculated in accordance with regulations.

(8) In this section—

"final relevant year" means the tax year immediately preceding that in which the pensioner attains pensionable age;

"state scheme pension debit", means a debit under section 49(1)(a) of the Welfare Reform and Pensions Act 1999 (debit for the purposes of this Part of this Act);

"valuation day" means the day on which the pensioner became subject to the state scheme pension debit.

55C   Increase of shared additional pension where entitlement is deferred

(1) For the purposes of this section, a person's entitlement to a shared additional pension is deferred—

(a)   where he would be entitled to a Category A or Category B retirement pension but for the fact that his entitlement to such a pension is deferred, if and so long as his entitlement to such a pension is deferred, and

(b)   otherwise, if and so long as he does not become entitled to the shared additional pension by reason only of not satisfying the conditions of section 1 of the Administration Act (entitlement to benefit dependent on claim),

and, in relation to a shared additional pension, "period of deferment" shall be construed accordingly.

(2) Where a person's entitlement to a shared additional pension is deferred, the rate of his shared additional pension shall be increased by an amount equal to the aggregate of the increments to which he is entitled under subsection (3) below, but only if that amount is enough to increase the rate of the pension by at least 1 per cent.

(3) A person is entitled to an increment under this subsection for each complete incremental period in his period of enhancement.

(4) The amount of the increment for an incremental period shall be 1/7th per cent. of the weekly rate of the shared additional pension to which the person would have been entitled for the period if his entitlement had not been deferred.

(5) Amounts under subsection (4) above shall be rounded to the nearest penny, taking any 1/2p as nearest to the next whole penny.

(6) Where an amount under subsection (4) above would, apart from this subsection, be a sum less than 1/2p, the amount shall be taken to be zero, notwithstanding any other provision of this Act, the Pensions Act 1995 or the Administration Act.

(7) Where one or more orders have come into force under section 150 of the Administration Act during the period of enhancement, the rate for any incremental period shall be determined as if the order or orders had come into force before the beginning of the period of enhancement.

(8) The sums which are the increases in the rates of shared additional pensions under this section are subject to alteration by order made by the Secretary of State under section 150 of the Administration Act.

(9) In this section—

"incremental period" means any period of six days which are treated by regulations as days of increment for the purposes of this section in relation to the person and pension in question; and "period of enhancement", in relation to that person and that pension, means the period which—

(a) begins on the same day as the period of deferment in question, and

(b) ends on the same day as that period or, if earlier, on the day before the 5th anniversary of the beginning of that period.'

. . .

SCHEDULE 12   Section 84

CONSEQUENTIAL AMENDMENTS

PART I

AMENDMENTS CONSEQUENTIAL ON PARTS III AND IV

Supreme Court Act 1981 (c 54)

1. In paragraph 3 of Schedule 1 to the Supreme Court Act 1981, after paragraph (f) there is inserted—

'(fa) all proceedings relating to a debit or credit under section 29(1) or 49(1) of the Welfare Reform and Pensions Act 1999;'.

Matrimonial and Family Proceedings Act 1984 (c 42)

2. The Matrimonial and Family Proceedings Act 1984 is amended as follows.

3. In section 17, for subsection (1) there is substituted—

'(1) Subject to section 20 below, on an application by a party to a marriage for an order for financial relief under this section, the court may—

(a) make any one or more of the orders which it could make under Part II of the 1973 Act if a decree of divorce, a decree of nullity of marriage or a decree of judicial separation in respect of the marriage had been granted in England and Wales, that is to say—

(i) any order mentioned in section 23(1) of the 1973 Act (financial provision orders); and

(ii) any order mentioned in section 24(1) of that Act (property adjustment orders); and

(b) if the marriage has been dissolved or annulled, make one or more orders each of which would, within the meaning of that Part of that Act, be a pension sharing order in relation to the marriage.'

4. In section 21—

(a) the word 'made' in both places, is omitted,

(b) after paragraph (b) there is inserted—

'(ba) section 24B(3) to (5) (provisions about pension sharing orders in relation to divorce and nullity);

(bb) section 24C (duty to stay pension sharing orders);

(bc) section 24D (apportionment of pension sharing charges);', and

(c) at the end there is inserted—

'(l) section 40A (appeals relating to pension sharing orders which have taken effect).'

Family Law (Scotland) Act 1985 (c 37)

5. The Family Law (Scotland) Act 1985 has effect subject to the following amendments.

6. In section 8, after subsection (3) there is inserted—

'(4) The court shall not, in the same proceedings, make both a pension sharing order and an order under section 12A(2) or (3) of this Act in relation to the same pension arrangement.

(5) Where, as regards a pension arrangement, the parties to a marriage have in effect a qualifying agreement which contains a term relating to pension sharing, the court shall not—

(a) make an order under section 12A(2) or (3) of this Act; or

(b) make a pension sharing order,

relating to the arrangement unless it also sets aside the agreement or term under section 16(1)(b) of this Act.

(6) The court shall not make a pension sharing order in relation to the rights of a person under a pension arrangement if there is in force an order under section 12A(2) or (3) of this Act which relates to benefits or future benefits to which he is entitled under the pension arrangement.

(7) In subsection (5) above—

(a) "term relating to pension sharing" shall be construed in accordance with section 16(2A) of this Act; and

(b) "qualifying agreement" has the same meaning as in section 28(3) of the Welfare Reform and Pensions Act 1999.'

7. After section 8 there is inserted—

'8A Pension sharing orders: apportionment of charges

If a pension sharing order relates to rights under a pension arrangement, the court may include in the order provision about the apportionment between the parties of any charge under section 41 of the Welfare Reform and Pensions Act 1999 (charges in respect of pension sharing costs) or under corresponding Northern Ireland legislation.'

8.—(1) Section 10 is amended as follows.

(2) In subsection (5)(b), for 'scheme' there is substituted 'arrangement'.

(3) For subsection (8) there is substituted—

'(8) The Secretary of State may by regulations make provision about calculation and verification in relation to the valuation for the purposes of this Act of benefits under a pension arrangement or relevant state scheme rights.'

(4) After that subsection there is inserted—

'(8A) Regulations under subsection (8) above may include—

(a) provision for calculation or verification in accordance with guidance from time to time prepared by a prescribed person; and

(b) provision by reference to regulations under section 30 or 49(4) of the Welfare Reform and Pensions Act 1999.'

(5) In subsection (9), after 'subsection (8) above' there is inserted 'may make different provision for different purposes and'.

(6) Subsections (10) and (11) cease to have effect.

9.—(1) Section 12A is amended as follows.

(2) In subsection (1)(a), for 'scheme' there is substituted 'arrangement'.

(3) In subsection (2), for 'trustees or managers of the pension scheme' there is substituted 'person responsible for the pension arrangement'.

(4) In subsection (3), in paragraphs (a) and (c) for 'trustees or managers of the pension scheme' there is substituted 'person responsible for the pension arrangement' and in paragraph (a) for 'have' there is substituted 'has'.

(5) In subsection (4)—

  (a) for 'trustees or managers' there is substituted 'person responsible for the pension arrangement', and
  (b) for 'trustees' or managers' liability' there is substituted 'liability of the person responsible for the pension arrangement'.

(6) In subsection (5), for 'trustees or managers' there is substituted 'person responsible for the pension arrangement'.

(7) In subsection (6)—

  (a) for 'trustees or managers of', wherever occurring, there is substituted 'person responsible for',
  (b) for 'scheme', wherever occurring, there is substituted 'arrangement', and
  (c) in paragraph (b), for 'have' there is substituted 'has'.

(8) In subsection (7)—

  (a) for 'trustees or managers' where first occurring there is substituted 'person responsible for the pension arrangement',
  (b) for 'trustees or managers of' there is substituted 'person responsible for', and
  (c) for 'scheme' there is substituted 'arrangement'.

(9) For subsection (10) there is substituted—

  '(10) The definition of "benefits under a pension scheme" in section 27 of this Act does not apply to this section.'

10. In section 13(2)(b), after 'propery' there is inserted ', or a pension sharing order,'.

11.—(1) Section 16 is amended as follows.

(2) In subsection (2), for paragraph (b) there is substituted—

  '(b) under subsection (1)(b) above, if the agreement does not contain a term relating to pension sharing, on granting decree of divorce or within such time as the court may specify on granting decree of divorce; or
  (c) under subsection (1)(b) above, if the agreement contains a term relating to pension sharing—

     (i)   where the order sets aside the agreement or sets aside or varies the term relating to pension sharing, on granting decree of divorce; and

    (ii)   where the order sets aside or varies any other term of the agreement, on granting decree of divorce or within such time thereafter as the court may specify on granting decree of divorce.'

(3) After that subsection there is inserted—

'(2A) In subsection (2) above, a term relating to pension sharing is a term corresponding to provision which may be made in a pension sharing order and satisfying the requirements set out in section 28(1)(f) or 48(1)(f) of the Welfare Reform and Pensions Act 1999.'

12. In section 27(1), the following definitions are inserted at the appropriate places—

'"benefits under a pension arrangement" includes any benefits by way of pension, including relevant state scheme rights, whether under a pension arrangement or not;'

'"pension arrangement" means—

    (a) any occupational pension scheme within the meaning of the Pension Schemes Act 1993;

    (b) a personal pension scheme within the meaning of that Act;

    (c) a retirement annuity contract;

    (d) an annuity or insurance policy purchased or transferred for the purpose of giving effect to rights under an occupational pension scheme or a personal pension scheme;

    (e) an annuity purchased or entered into for the purpose of discharging liability in respect of a pension credit under section 29(1)(b) of the Welfare Reform and Pensions Act 1999 or under corresponding Northern Ireland legislation;'

'"person responsible for a pension arrangement" means—

    (a) in the case of an occupational pension scheme or a personal pension scheme, the trustees or managers of the scheme;

    (b) in the case of a retirement annuity contract or an annuity falling within paragraph (d) or (e) of the definition of "pension arrangement" above, the provider of the annuity;

    (c) in the case of an insurance policy falling within paragraph (d) of the definition of that expression, the insurer;'

'"relevant state scheme rights" means—

   (a) entitlement, or prospective entitlement, to a Category A retire-
       ment pension by virtue of section 44(3)(b) of the Social Security
       Contributions and Benefits Act 1992 or under corresponding
       Northern Ireland legislation; and
   (b) entitlement, or prospective entitlement, to a pension under
       section 55A of the Social Security Contributions and Benefits Act
       1992 (shared additional pension) or under corresponding North-
       ern Ireland legislation;'

'"retirement annuity contract" means a contract or scheme approved under
Chapter III of Part XIV of the Income and Corporation Taxes Act 1988;'

'"trustees or managers" in relation to an occupational pension scheme or a
personal pension scheme means—

   (a) in the case of a scheme established under a trust, the trustees of the
       scheme; and
   (b) in any other case, the managers of the scheme;'

Income and Corporation Taxes Act 1988 (c 1)

13. In section 659D(2) of the Income and Corporation Taxes Act 1988, for
'24(1)' there is substituted '28(1)'.

Social Security Contributions and Benefits Act 1992 (c 4)

14. The Contributions and Benefits Act has effect subject to the following
amendments.

15.—(1) Section 20 is amended as follows.

(2) In subsection (1), after paragraph (f) there is inserted—

   '(fa) shared additional pensions;'.

(3) In subsection (2), in the definition of "long-term benefit", after
paragraph (d) there is inserted—

   '(e) a shared additional pension;'.

16. In section 21(1), after '41 below' there is inserted 'or a shared additional
pension under section 55A below'.

17. In section 39(1), (2) and (3), for '45A' there is substituted '45B'.

18. In section 43, at the end there is inserted—

'(6) For the purposes of this section, a pension under section 55A below is not a retirement pension.'

19. In section 48A(4), for '45A' there is substituted '45B'.

20. In section 48B(2) and (3), for '45A' there is substituted '45B'.

21. In section 48C(4), for '45A' there is substituted '45B'.

22. In section 54(1), at the end there is inserted 'or to a shared additional pension'.

Social Security Administration Act 1992 (c 5)

23. The Administration Act is amended as follows.

24. In section 150(1)—

  (a) after paragraph (c) there is inserted—
     '(ca) which are shared additional pensions;', and
  (b) after paragraph (d) there is inserted—
     '(da) which are the increases in the rates of shared additional pensions under section 55C of that Act;'.

25.—(1) Section 155A is amended as follows.

(2) In subsection (1)(a)(i), after 'retirement pension' there is inserted 'or shared additional pension'.

(3) In subsection (2), after 'retirement pension' there is inserted ', a shared additional pension'.

26. In section 163(2)—

  (a) after paragraph (a) there is inserted—
     '(aa) any administrative expenses of the Secretary of State in supplying information about benefits under Part II of that Act in accordance with regulations under section 23 of the Welfare Reform and Pensions Act 1999;', and
  (b) in paragraph (b), for 'that Act' there is substituted 'the Contributions and Benefits Act'.

27. In section 165(5)(b), after 'section 163(2)(a)' there is inserted 'or (aa)'.

Pensions Schemes Act 1993 (c 48)

28. The Pension Schemes Act 1993 has effect subject to the following amendments.

29. In section 50(1)—

  (a) in paragraph (a), at the end there is inserted—
       '(iii) of safeguarded rights under the scheme;'
  (b) in paragraph (b), after 'protected' there is inserted ', or safeguarded,'.

30.—(1) Section 52 is amended as follows.

(2) In subsection (2A), at the end there is inserted—

  '(c) any persons who have safeguarded rights under the scheme or are entitled to any benefit giving effect to safeguarded rights under it.'

(3) In subsection (3)(b), after 'protected', in both places, there is inserted ', or safeguarded,'.

31.—(1) Section 83 is amended as follows.

(2) In subsection (1), before 'benefits', in both places, there is inserted 'relevant'.

(3) After that subsection there is inserted—

  '(1A) The following are relevant benefits for the purposes of subsection (1)—
     (a) any benefits payable otherwise than by virtue of rights which are attributable (directly or indirectly) to a pension credit, and
     (b) in the case of a salary related occupational pension scheme, any benefits payable by virtue of such rights, to the extent that the rights involve the member being credited by the scheme with notional pensionable service.'

(4) At the end there is inserted—

  '(4) For the purposes of this section, an occupational pension scheme is salary related if—
     (a) it is not a money purchase scheme, and
     (b) it does not fall within a prescribed class.'

32. In section 85, after '73(2)(b)' there is inserted 'or 101D(2)(b)'.

33. In section 93, after subsection (1) there is inserted—

  '(1ZA) In subsection (1), references to accrued rights to benefit do not include rights which are attributable (directly or indirectly) to a pension credit.'

34. In section 93A, after subsection (1) there is inserted—

'(1A) In subsection (1), the reference to benefits which have accrued does not include benefits which are attributable (directly or indirectly) to a pension credit.'

35. In section 94, after subsection (1A) there is inserted—

'(1B) In subsection (1), references to benefits which have accrued do not include benefits which are attributable (directly or indirectly) to a pension credit.'

36. In section 96, there is inserted at the end—

'(4) Where a member of an occupational pension scheme or a personal pension scheme—
   (a) is entitled to give a notice under section 101F(1) to the trustees or managers of the scheme, or
   (b) would be entitled to do so, but for section 101G(1),
he may not, if the scheme so provides, make an application to them under section 95 unless he also gives them a notice under section 101F(1).'

37.—(1) Section 98 is amended as follows.

(2) In subsection (5)—

   (a) after 'part of the' there is inserted 'relevant', and
   (b) for 'any of the benefits mentioned in that section' there is substituted 'benefits'.

(3) In subsection (8), after 'this section' there is inserted—

'"relevant benefits" means any benefits not attributable (directly or indirectly) to a pension credit; and'.

38.—(1) Section 100 is amended as follows.

(2) In subsection (1), for 'subsection (2)' there is substituted 'subsections (2) and (2A)'.

(3) After subsection (2) there is inserted—

'(2A) If the making of the application depended on the giving of a notice under section 101F(1), the application may only be withdrawn if the notice is also withdrawn.'

39.—(1) Section 129 is amended as follows.

(2) In subsection (1), after 'Part IV,' there is inserted 'Chapters I and II of Part IVA,'.

(3) In subsection (2), for 'does' there is substituted 'and Chapter II of Part IVA do'.

40.—(1) Section 178 is amended as follows.

(2) In paragraph (a)—

   (a)   the words 'or of' are omitted, and
   (b)   at the end there is inserted ', section 25D of the Matrimonial Causes Act 1973, section 12A of the Family Law (Scotland) Act 1985 or Part III or IV of the Welfare Reform and Pensions Act 1999.'

(3) In paragraph (b), after 'Part IV,' there is inserted 'Chapter I of Part IVA,'.

41. In section 181(1)—

   (a)   after the definition of 'occupational pension scheme' there is inserted—

   '"pension credit" means a credit under section 29(1)(b) of the Welfare Reform and Pensions Act 1999 or under corresponding Northern Ireland legislation;', and

   (b)   after the definition of 'rights' there is inserted—

   '"safeguarded rights" has the meaning given in section 68A;'.

42. In section 183(3), for 'and 97(1)' there is substituted ', 97(1) and 101I'.

Pensions Act 1995 (c 26)

43. The Pensions Act 1995 has effect subject to the following amendments.

44. In section 3(2)(a)—

   (a)   in sub-paragrpah (ii), after 'values),' there is inserted 'Chapter II of Part IVA (pension credit benefit transfer values),', and
   (b)   after that sub-paragraph there is inserted 'or
      (iii)   the following provisions of the Welfare Reform and Pensions Act 1999: section 33 (time for discharge of pension credit liability) and section 45 (information),'.

45.—(1) Section 16 is amended as follows.

(2) In subsections (1)(a) and (6)(a), before 'members' there is inserted 'qualifying'.

(3) In subsection (8)—

    (a) after 'a', in the second place, there is inserted 'qualifying', and

    (b) for 'a member of the scheme', in the second place, there is substituted 'such a member'.

46. In section 17(4)(a), before 'members' there is inserted 'qualifying'.

47.—(1) Section 18 is amended as follows.

(2) In subsections (1)(a) and (6)(a), before 'members' there is inserted 'qualifying'.

(3) In subsection (7)—

    (a) after 'a', in the second place, there is inserted 'qualifying', and

    (b) for 'a member of the scheme', in the second place, there is substituted 'such a member'.

48. In section 20(5), after 'a', in the second place, there is inserted 'qualifying'.

49. In section 21(7)—

    (a) after 'section' there is inserted—
        '(a) "qualifying member", in relation to a trust scheme, means a person who is an active, deferred or pensioner member of the scheme, and
        (b)',
        and

    (b) before 'members' there is inserted 'qualifying'.

50.—(1) Section 38 is amended as follows.

(2) In subsection (1), for the words from 'that the scheme' to the end there is substituted—

    '(a) that the scheme is not for the time being to be wound up but that no new members are to be admitted to it, or

    (b) that the scheme is not for the time being to be wound up but that no new members, except pension credit members, are to be admitted to it.'

(3) In subsection (2), the words from 'but' to the end are omitted.

(4) After that subsection there is inserted—

    '(2A) Subsection (2) does not authorise the trustees to determine—
        (a) where there are accrued rights or pension credit rights to any benefit, that the benefit is not to be increased, or

(b)   where the power conferred by that subsection is exercisable by virtue of a determination under subsection (1)(b), that members of the scheme may not acquire pension credit rights under it.'

51. In section 51(6), after 'a pension' there is inserted 'which is attributable (directly or indirectly) to a pension credit or'.

52. In section 53, after subsection (3) there is inserted—

'(3A) In subsections (1) and (2), the references to a person's pension do not include any pension which is attributable (directly or indirectly) to a pension credit.'

53.—(1) Section 67 is amended as follows.

(2) In subsection (2), for 'or accrued right,' there is substituted 'accrued right or pension credit right'.

(3) In subsection (4)(a), for 'or accrued rights,' there is substituted 'accrued rights or pension credit rights'.

(4) For subsection (5) there is substituted—

'(5) Subsection (2) does not apply to the exercise of a power—
(a)   for a purpose connected with debits under section 29(1)(a) of the Welfare Reform and Pensions Act 1999, or
(b)   in a prescribed manner.'

54. In section 68(2), for 'and' at the end of paragraph (d) there is substituted—

'(da) to enable the scheme to accommodate persons with pension credits or pension credit rights, and'.

55. In section 73, after subsection (3) there is inserted—

'(3A) No pension or other benefit which is attributable (directly or indirectly) to a pension credit may be regarded for the purposes of subsection (3)(a) as derived from the payment of voluntary contributions.'

56. In section 74(3)(b), at the end there is inserted 'or pension credit rights'.

57.—(1) Section 91 is amended as follows.

(2) In subsection (1), for the words from ', or has' to 'occupational pension scheme' there is substituted 'to a pension under an occupational pension scheme or has a right to a future pension under such a scheme'.

(3) In subsection (2), for the words from ', or' to 'scheme' there is substituted 'to a pension under an occupational pension scheme, or right to a future pension under such a scheme,'.

(4) In subsection (5)—

(a) for the words from ', or has' to 'scheme' there is substituted 'to a pension under an occupational pension scheme, or has a right to a future pension under such a scheme',

(b) in paragraph (d), for 'accrued right, to pension' there is substituted 'right', and

(c) in paragraph (e), for 'accrued right, to pension' there is substituted 'right'.

58.—(1) Section 92 is amended as follows.

(2) In subsection (1), for the words from ', or' to 'scheme' there is substituted 'to a pension under an occupational pension scheme or a right to a future pension under such a scheme'.

(3) In subsection (4), for the words from 'person entitled' to 'accrued' there is substituted 'pensioner, or prospective pensioner'.

59.—(1) Section 93 is amended as follows.

(2) In subsection (1), for the words from ', or' to 'scheme' there is substituted 'to a pension under an occupational pension scheme or right to a future pension under such a scheme'.

(3) In subsection (2)—

(a) for 'accrued right to a pension' there is substituted 'right', and

(b) for 'accrued right to a pension under the scheme' there is substituted 'right'.

(4) In subsection (4), for 'accrued right to a pension' there is substituted 'right'.

60. In section 99(2)—

(a) in paragraph (b), after 'values),' there is inserted 'Chapter II of Part IVA (pension credit benefit transfer values),', and

(b) at the end of that paragraph there is inserted—

'(ba) section 33 (time for discharge of pension credit liability) or 45 (information) of the Welfare Reform and Pensions Act 1999,'.

61.—(1) Section 124 is amended as follows.

(2) In subsection (1), in the definition of 'member', for 'or pensioner' there is substituted ', pensioner or pension credit'.

(3) In that subsection, after the definition of 'payment schedule' there is inserted—

'"pension credit" means a credit under section 29(1)(b) of the Welfare Reform and Pensions Act 1999 or under corresponding Northern Ireland legislation,

"pension credit member", in relation to an occupational pension scheme, means a person who has rights under the scheme which are attributable (directly or indirectly) to a pension credit,

"pension credit rights", in relation to an occupational pension scheme, means rights to future benefits under the scheme which are attributable (directly or indirectly) to a pension credit,'.

(4) After subsection (2) there is inserted—

'(2A) In subsection (2)(a), the reference to rights which have accrued to or in respect of the member does not include any rights which are pension credit rights.'

62.—(1) Section 166 is amended as follows.

(2) In subsection (4), for 'scheme' there is substituted 'arrangement'.

(3) In subsection (5)(d), for 'scheme' there is substituted 'arrangement'.

63. In section 167(4)—

(a) for 'scheme', where first occurring, there is substituted 'arrangement', and

(b) for the words from '"pension scheme"' to the end of the subsection there is substituted '"pension arrangement" having the meaning given in subsection (1) of section 27 of that Act, as it has effect for the purposes of subsection (5) of the said section 10).'

Family Law Act 1996 (c 27)

64. The Family Law Act 1996 has effect subject to the following amendments.

65.—(1) Schedule 2 is amended as follows.

(2) In paragraph 2, for 'section 21' there is substituted 'sections 21 and 21A'.

(3) In the section set out in that paragraph, for the sidenote there is substituted 'Financial provision orders, property adjustment orders and pension sharing orders.'

(4) In that section, in paragraphs (c) and (d) of subsection (2), there is inserted at the end ', other than one in the form of a pension arrangement (within the meaning of section 25D below)'.

(5) In that section, after subsection (2) there is inserted—

'(3) For the purposes of this Act, a pension sharing order is an order which—
  (a) provides that one party's—
    (i) shareable rights under a specified pension arrangement, or
    (ii) shareable state scheme rights,
    be subject to pension sharing for the benefit of the other party, and
  (b) specifies the percentage value to be transferred.'

(6) In that section, subsections (3), (4) and (5) become (4), (5) and (6).

(7) In that section, after subsection (6) (new numbering) there is inserted—

'(7) In subsection (3)—

  (a) the reference to shareable rights under a pension arrangement is to rights in relation to which pension sharing is available under Chapter I of Part IV of the Welfare Reform and Pensions Act 1999, or under corresponding Northern Ireland legislation, and
  (b) the reference to shareable state scheme rights is to rights in relation to which pension sharing is available under Chapter II of Part IV of the Welfare Reform and Pensions Act 1999, or under corresponding Northern Ireland legislation.'

(8) In that section, subsection (6) becomes subsection (8).

(9) After paragraph 6 there is inserted—

'Pension sharing orders: divorce and nullity

6A　For section 24B substitute—

"24B　Pension sharing orders: divorce

(1) On an application made under this section, the court may at the appropriate time make one or more pension sharing orders.

(2) The 'appropriate time' is any time—

    (a)　after a statement of marital breakdown has been received by the court and before any application for a divorce order or for a separation order is made to the court by reference to that statement;

    (b)　when an application for a divorce order has been made under section 3 of the 1996 Act and has not been withdrawn;

    (c)　when an application for a divorce order has been made under section 4 of the 1996 Act and has not been withdrawn;

    (d)　after a divorce order has been made.

(3) The court shall exercise its powers under this section, so far as is practicable, by making on one occasion all such provision as can be made by way of one or more pension sharing orders in relation to the marriage as it thinks fit.

(4) This section is to be read subject to any restrictions imposed by this Act and to section 19 of the 1996 Act.

24BA　Restrictions affecting section 24B

(1) No pension sharing order may be made under section 24B above so as to take effect before the making of a divorce order in relation to the marriage.

(2) The court may not make a pension sharing order under section 24B above at any time while the period for reflection and consideration is interrupted under section 7(8) of the 1996 Act.

(3) No pension sharing order may be made under section 24B above by virtue of a statement of marital breakdown if, by virtue of section 5(3) or 7(9) of the 1996 Act (lapse of divorce process), it has ceased to be possible—

    (a)　for an application to be made by reference to that statement, or

    (b)　for an order to be made on such an application.

(4) No pension sharing order may be made under section 24B above after a divorce order has been made, except—

   (a)   in response to an application made before the divorce order was made, or
   (b)   on a subsequent application made with the leave of the court.

(5) A pension sharing order under section 24B above may not be made in relation to a pension arrangement which—

   (a)   is the subject of a pension sharing order in relation to the marriage, or
   (b)   has been the subject of pension sharing between the parties to the marriage.

(6) A pension sharing order under section 24B above may not be made in relation to shareable state scheme rights if—

   (a)   such rights are the subject of a pension sharing order in relation to the marriage, or
   (b)   such rights have been the subject of pension sharing between the parties to the marriage.

(7) A pension sharing order under section 24B above may not be made in relation to the rights of a person under a pension arrangement if there is in force a requirement imposed by virtue of section 25B or 25C below which relates to benefits or future benefits to which he is entitled under the pension arrangement.

(8) In this section, 'period for reflection and consideration' means the period fixed by section 7 of the 1996 Act.

24BB   Pension sharing orders: nullity of marriage

(1) On or after granting a decree of nullity of marriage (whether before or after the decree is made absolute), the court may, on an application made under this section, make one or more pension sharing orders in relation to the marriage.

(2) The court shall exercise its powers under this section, so far as is practicable, by making on one occasion all such provision as can be made by way of one or more pension sharing orders in relation to the marriage as it thinks fit.

(3) Where a pension sharing order is made under this section on or after the granting of a decree of nullity of marriage, the order is not to take effect unless the decree has been made absolute.

(4) This section is to be read subject to any restrictions imposed by this Act.

24BC   Restrictions affecting section 24BB

(1) A pension sharing order under section 24BB above may not be made in relation to a pension arrangement which—

    (a) is the subject of a pension sharing order in relation to the marriage, or

    (b) has been the subject of pension sharing between the parties to the marriage.

(2) A pension sharing order under section 24BB above may not be made in relation to shareable state scheme rights if—

    (a) such rights are the subject of a pension sharing order in relation to the marriage, or

    (b) such rights have been the subject of pension sharing between the parties to the marriage.

(3) A pension sharing order under section 24BB above may not be made in relation to the rights of a person under a pension arrangement if there is in force a requirement imposed by virtue of section 25B or 25C below which relates to benefits or future benefits to which he is entitled under the pension arrangement."'

66.—(1) Schedule 8 is amended as follows.

(2) In paragraph 9—

    (a) in sub-paragraph (2)—
        (i)   for 'or 24A' there is substituted ', 24A or 24B', and
        (ii)   for 'to 24A' there is substituted 'to 24BB', and
    (b) in sub-paragraph (3), after paragraph (a) there is inserted—
      '(aa) for "or 24B" substitute ", 24B or 24BB",'.

(3) In paragraph 10, in sub-paragraph (2), for '24A' there is substituted '24BB'.

(4) For paragraph 11 there is substituted—

    '11. In each of sections 25B(3) and 25C(1) and (3), for "sections 23" substitute "section 22A or 23".

    11A. In section 25D—

  (a) in each subsections (1)(a) and (2)(a) and (ab), for "section 23" substitute "section 22A or 23", and

  (b) in subsection (3), in the definition of "shareable state scheme rights", for "section 21A(1)" substitute "section 21(3)".'

(5) In paragraph 16, in sub-paragraph (2), at the end there is inserted—

  '(f) after paragraph (f) there is inserted—
   "(fa) a pension sharing order under section 24B which is made at a time when no divorce order has been made, and no separation order is in force, in relation to the marriage;"

  (g) in paragraph (g), for "24B" substitute "24BB".'

(6) In that paragraph, after sub-paragraph (3) there is inserted—

  '(3A) In subsection (4A), after "paragraph" insert "(de), (ea), (fa) or".'

(7) In that paragraph, in sub-paragraph (4), for the words from 'subsection (4)' to the end of the first of the inserted subsections there is substituted 'subsection (4A) insert—', the second of the inserted subsections is renumbered '(4AA)' and after that subsection there is inserted—

  '(4AB) No variation of a pension sharing order under section 24B above shall be made so as to take effect before the making of a divorce order in relation to the marriage.'

(8) In that paragraph, after sub-paragraph (4) there is inserted—

  '(4A) In subsection (4B), after "order" insert "under section 24BB above".'

(9) In that paragraph, after sub-paragraph (7) there is inserted—

  '(8) After subsection (7F) insert—
   "(7FA) Section 24B(3) above applies where the court makes a pension sharing order under subsection (7B) above as it applies where the court makes such an order under section 24B above."

  (9) In subsection (7G)—
   (a) for "Subsections (3) to (5) of section 24B" substitute "Section 24BA(5) to (7)", and
   (b) for "that section" substitute "section 24B above".'

(10) After that paragraph there is inserted—

  '16A. After section 31A insert—

"31B   Discharge of pension sharing orders on making of separation order

Where, after the making of a pension sharing order under section 24B above in relation to a marriage, a separation order is made in relation to the marriage, the pension sharing order is discharged." '

(11) In paragraph 19, in sub-paragraph (3)—

- (a) after '24A' there is inserted ', 24B', and
- (b) after 'property adjustment order,' there is inserted 'any pension sharing order,'.

(12) In paragraph 21—

- (a) after '24,', in the first place, there is inserted '24B,', and
- (b) for '24,', in the second place, there is substituted '24BB,'.

(13) After paragraph 25 there is inserted—

'25A. In section 52(2)(aa), for "section 21A" substitute "section 21".'

(14) In paragraph 32, in sub-paragraph (2), for the words from 'the words' to the end there is substituted 'paragraph (a) substitute—

"(a) make one or more orders each of which would, within the meaning of Part II of the 1973 Act, be a financial provision order in favour of a party to the marriage or a child of the family or a property adjustment order in relation to the marriage,".'

(15) In that paragraph, in sub-paragraph (3), for '21(a)' there is substituted '21(1)(a)'.

(16) In that paragraph, after sub-paragraph (3) there is inserted—

'(3A) For section 21(1)(ba) substitute—
          "(ba) sections 24BA(5) to (7) (provisions about pension shar-
                  ing orders in relation to divorce);
          (baa) section 24BC(1) to (3) (provisions about pension sharing
                  orders in relation to nullity),".
(3B) In section 21(3), for "section 23" substitute "section 22A or 23".'

(17) At the end of Part I insert—

'The Welfare Reform and Pensions Act 1999

43A. In section 24 of the Welfare Reform and Pensions Act 1999 (charges by pension arrangements in relation to earmarking orders), for "section 23" substitute "section 22A or 23".'

PART II

OTHER CONSEQUENTIAL AMENDMENTS

Bankruptcy (Scotland) Act 1985 (c 66)

67. The Bankruptcy (Scotland) Act 1985 has effect subject to the following amendments.

68. In section 35(1), in paragraph (a) for 'under the said section 8(2) for the transfer of property by him' substitute 'a court has, under the said section 8(2), made an order for the transfer of property by him or made a pension sharing order'.

69. After section 36C there is inserted—

'36D   Recovery of excessive contributions in pension-sharing cases

(1) For the purposes of section 34 of this Act, a pension-sharing transaction shall be taken—

(a)   to be a transaction, entered into by the transferor with the transferee, by which the appropriate amount is transferred by the transferor to the transferee; and

(b)   to be capable of being an alienation challengeable under that section only so far as it is a transfer of so much of the appropriate amount as is recoverable.

(2) For the purposes of section 35 of this Act, a pension-sharing transaction shall be taken—

(a)   to be a pension sharing order made by the court under section 8(2) of the Family Law (Scotland) Act 1985; and

(b)   to be an order capable of being recalled under that section only so far as it is a payment or transfer of so much of the appropriate amount as is recoverable.

(3) For the purposes of section 36 of this Act, a pension-sharing transaction shall be taken—

(a) to be something (namely a transfer of the appropriate amount to the transferee) done by the transferor; and

(b) to be capable of being an unfair preference given to the transferee only so far as it is a transfer of so much of the appropriate amount as is recoverable.

(4) Where—

(a) an alienation is challenged under section 34;

(b) an application is made under section 35 for the recall of an order made in divorce proceedings; or

(c) a transaction is challenged under section 36,

if any question arises as to whether, or the extent to which, the appropriate amount in the case of a pension-sharing transaction is recoverable, the question shall be determined in accordance with subsections (5) to (9).

(5) The court shall first determine the extent (if any) to which the transferor's rights under the shared arrangement at the time of the transaction appear to have been (whether directly or indirectly) the fruits of contributions ("personal contributions")—

(a) which the transferor has at any time made on his own behalf, or

(b) which have at any time been made on the transferor's behalf,

to the shared arrangement or any other pension arrangement.

(6) Where it appears that those rights were to any extent the fruits of personal contributions, the court shall then determine the extent (if any) to which those rights appear to have been the fruits of personal contributions whose making has unfairly prejudiced the transferor's creditors ("the unfair contributions").

(7) If it appears to the court that the extent to which those rights were the fruits of the unfair contributions is such that the transfer of the appropriate amount could have been made out of rights under the shared arrangement which were not the fruits of the unfair contributions, then the appropriate amount is not recoverable.

(8) If it appears to the court that the transfer could not have been wholly so made, then the appropriate amount is recoverable to the extent to which it appears to the court that the transfer could not have been so made.

(9) In making the determination mentioned in subsection (6) the court shall consider in particular—

(a) whether any of the personal contributions were made for the purpose of putting assets beyond the reach of the transferor's creditors or any of them; and

(b) whether the total amount of any personal contributions represented, at the time the pension sharing arrangement was made, by rights under pension arrangements is an amount which is excessive in view of the transferor's circumstances when those contributions were made.

(10) In this section and sections 36E and 36F—

"appropriate amount", in relation to a pension-sharing transaction, means the appropriate amount in relation to that transaction for the purposes of section 29(1) of the Welfare Reform and Pensions Act 1999 (creation of pension credits and debits);

"pension-sharing transaction" means an order or provision falling within section 28(1) of the Welfare Reform and Pensions Act 1999 orders and agreements which activate pension-sharing);

"shared arrangement", in relation to a pension-sharing transaction, means the pension arrangement to which the transaction relates;

"transferee", in relation to a pension-sharing transaction, means the person for whose benefit the transaction is made;

"transferor", in relation to a pension-sharing transaction, means the person to whose rights the transaction relates.

36E Recovery orders

(1) In this section and section 36F of this Act, "recovery order" means—

(a) a decree granted under section 34(4) of this Act;
(b) an order made under section 35(2) of this Act;
(c) a decree granted under section 36(5) of this Act,

in any proceedings to which section 36D of this Act applies.

(2) Without prejudice to the generality of section 34(4), 35(2) or 36(5) a recovery order may include provision—

(a) requiring the person responsible for a pension arrangement in which the transferee has acquired rights derived directly or indirectly from the pension-sharing transaction to pay an amount to the permanent trustee,

(b) adjusting the liabilities of the pension arrangement in respect of the transferee,

(c) adjusting any liabilities of the pension arrangement in respect of any other person that derive, directly or indirectly, from rights of the transferee under the arrangement,

(d) for the recovery by the person responsible for the pension arrangement (whether by deduction from any amount which that person is ordered to pay or otherwise) of costs incurred by that person in complying in the debtor's case with any requirement under section 36F(1) or in giving effect to the order.

(3) In subsection (2), references to adjusting the liabilities of a pension arrangement in respect of a person include (in particular) reducing the amount of any benefit or future benefit to which that person is entitled under the arrangement.

(4) The maximum amount which the person responsible for an arrangement may be required to pay by a recovery order is the smallest of—

(a) so much of the appropriate amount as, in accordance with section 36D of this Act, is recoverable,

(b) so much (if any) of the amount of the unfair contributions (within the meaning given by section 36D(6)) as is not recoverable by way of an order under section 36A of this Act containing provision such as is mentioned in section 36B(1)(a), and

(c) the value of the debtor's rights under the arrangement acquired by the transferee as a consequence of the transfer of the appropriate amount.

(5) A recovery order which requires the person responsible for an arrangement to pay an amount ("the restoration amount") to the permanent trustee must provide for the liabilities of the arrangement to be correspondingly reduced.

(6) For the purposes of subsection (5), liabilities are correspondingly reduced if the difference between—

(a) the amount of the liabilities immediately before the reduction, and

(b) the amount of the liabilities immediately after the reduction, is equal to the restoration amount.

(7) A recovery order in respect of an arrangement—

- (a) shall be binding on the person responsible for the arrangement, and
- (b) overrides provisions of the arrangement to the extent that they conflict with the provisions of the order.

36F   Recovery orders: supplementary

(1) The person responsible for a pension arrangement under which the transferee has, at any time, acquired rights by virtue of the transfer of the appropriate amount shall, on the permanent trustee making a written request, provide the trustee with such information about the arrangement and the rights under it of the transferor and transferee as the permanent trustee may reasonably require for, or in connection with, the making of an application for a recovery order.

(2) Nothing in—

- (a) any provision of section 159 of the Pension Schemes Act 1993 or section 91 of the Pensions Act 1995 (which prevent assignation and the making of orders which restrain a person from receiving anything which he is prevented from assigning),
- (b) any provision of any enactment (whether passed or made before or after the passing of the Welfare Reform and Pensions Act 1999) corresponding to any of the provisions mentioned in paragraph (a), or
- (c) any provision of the arrangement in question corresponding to any of those provisions,

applies to a court exercising its power to make a recovery order.

(3) Regulations may, for the purposes of the recovery provisions, make provision about the calculation and verification of—

- (a) any such value as is mentioned in section 36E(4)(c);
- (b) any such amounts as are mentioned in section 36E(6)(a) and (b).

(4) The power conferred by subsection (3) includes power to provide for calculation or verification—

- (a) in such manner as may, in the particular case, be approved by a prescribed person; or
- (b) in accordance with guidance—

(i)   from time to time prepared by a prescribed person, and
(ii)   approved by the Secretary of State.

(5) References in the recovery provisions to the person responsible for a pension arrangement are to—

(a)   the trustees, managers or provider of the arrangement, or
(b)   the person having functions in relation to the arrangement corresponding to those of a trustee, manager or provider.

(6) In this section—

"prescribed" means prescribed by regulations;

"the recovery provisions" means this section and sections 34, 35, 36 and 36E of this Act;

"regulations" means regulations made by the Secretary of State.

(7) Regulations under the recovery provisions may—

(a)   make different provision for different cases;
(b)   contain such incidental, supplemental and transitional provisions as appear to the Secretary of State necessary or expedient.

(8) Regulations under the recovery provisions shall be made by statutory instrument subject to annulment in pursuance of a resolution of either House of Parliament.'

Insolvency Act 1986 (c 45)

70. The Insolvency Act 1986 is amended as follows.

71. After section 342C there is inserted—

'342D   Recovery of excessive contributions in pension-sharing cases

(1) For the purposes of sections 339, 341 and 342, a pension-sharing transaction shall be taken—

(a)   to be a transaction, entered into by the transferor with the transferee, by which the appropriate amount is transferred by the transferor to the transferee; and
(b)   to be capable of being a transaction entered into at an undervalue only so far as it is a transfer of so much of the appropriate amount as is recoverable.

(2) For the purposes of sections 340 to 342, a pension-sharing transaction shall be taken—

   (a)   to be something (namely a transfer of the appropriate amount to the transferee) done by the transferor; and
   (b)   to be capable of being a preference given to the transferee only so far as it is a transfer of so much of the appropriate amount as is recoverable.

(3) If on an application under section 339 or 340 any question arises as to whether, or the extent to which, the appropriate amount in the case of a pension-sharing transaction is recoverable, the question shall be determined in accordance with subsections (4) to (8).

(4) The court shall first determine the extent (if any) to which the transferor's rights under the shared arrangement at the time of the transaction appear to have been (whether directly or indirectly) the fruits of contributions ("personal contributions")—

   (a)   which the transferor has at any time made on his own behalf, or
   (b)   which have at any time been made on the transferor's behalf,

to the shared arrangement or any other pension arrangement.

(5) Where it appears that those rights were to any extent the fruits of personal contributions, the court shall then determine the extent (if any) to which those rights appear to have been the fruits of personal contributions whose making has unfairly prejudiced the transferor's creditors ("the unfair contributions").

(6) If it appears to the court that the extent to which those rights were the fruits of the unfair contributions is such that the transfer of the appropriate amount could have been made out of righs under the shared arrangement which were not the fruits of the unfair contri-butions, then the appropriate amount is not recoverable.

(7) If it appears to the court that the transfer could not have been wholly so made, then the appropriate amount is recoverable to the extent to which it appears to the court that the transfer could not have been so made.

(8) In making the determination mentioned in subsection (5) the court shall consider in particular—

   (a)   whether any of the personal contributions were made for the purpose of putting assets beyond the reach of the transferor's creditors or any of them, and

(b) whether the total amount of any personal contributions represented, at the time the pension-sharing transaction was made,
by rights under pension arrangements is an amount which is
excessive in view of the transferor's circumstances when those
contributions were made.

(9) In this section and sections 342E and 342F—

"appropriate amount", in relation to a pension-sharing transaction,
means the appropriate amount in relation to that transaction for the
purposes of section 29(1) of the Welfare Reform and Pensions Act 1999
(creation of pension credits and debits);

"pension-sharing transaction" means an order or provision falling
within section 28(1) of the Welfare Reform and Pensions Act 1999
(orders and agreements which activate pension-sharing);

"shared arrangement", in relation to a pension-sharing transaction,
means the pension arrangement to which the transaction relates;

"transferee", in relation to a pension-sharing transaction, means the
person for whose benefit the transacton is made;

"transferor", in relation to a pension-sharing transaction, means the
person to whose rights the transaction relates.

342E Orders under section 339 or 340 in respect of pension-sharing transactions

(1) This section and section 342F apply if the court is making an order
under section 339 or 340 in a case where—

(a) the transaction or preference is, or is any part of, a pension-
sharing transaction, and
(b) the transferee has rights under a pension arrangement ("the
destination arrangement", which may be the shared arrangement or any other pension arrangement) that are derived,
directly or indirectly, from the pension-sharing transaction.

(2) Without prejudice to the generality of section 339(2) or 340(2), or
of section 342, the order may include provision—

(a) requiring the person responsible for the destination arrangement to pay an amount to the transferor's trustee in bankruptcy,
(b) adjusting the liabilities of the destination arangement in respect
of the transferee,

(c)   adjusting any liabilities of the destination arrangement in respect of any other person that derive, directly or indirectly, from rights of the transferee under the destination arrangement,

(d)   for the recovery by the person responsible for the destination arrangement (whether by deduction from any amount which that person is ordered to pay or otherwise) of costs incurred by that person in complying in the transferor's case with any requirement under section 342F(1) or in giving effect to the order,

(e)   for the recovery, from the transferor's trustee in bankruptcy, by the person responsible for a pension arrangement, of costs incurred by that person in complying in the transferor's case with any requirement under section 342F(2) or (3).

(3) In subsection (2), references to adjusting the liablities of the destination arrangement in respect of a person include (in particular) reducing the amount of any benefit or future benefit to which that person is entitled under the arrangement.

(4) The maximum amount which the person responsible for the destination arrangement may be required to pay by the order is the smallest of—

(a)   so much of the appropriate amount as, in accordance with section 342D, is recoverable,

(b)   so much (if any) of the amount of the unfair contributions (within the meaning given by section 342D(5)) as is not recoverable by way of an order under section 342A containing provision such as is mentioned in section 342B(1)(a), and

(c)   the value of the transferee's rights under the destination arrangement so far as they are derived, directly or indirectly, from the pension-sharing transaction.

(5) If the order requires the person responsible for the destination arrangement to pay an amount ("the restoration amount") to the transferor's trustee in bankruptcy it must provide for the liabilities of the arrangement to be correspondingly reduced.

(6) For the purposes of subsection (5), liabilities are correspondingly reduced if the difference between—

(a)   the amount of the liabilities immediately before the reduction, and

(b)   the amount of the liabilities immediately after the reduction, is equal to the restoration amount.

(7) The order—

(a) shall be binding on the person responsible for the destination arrangement, and

(b) overrides provisions of the destination arrangement to the extent that they conflict with the provisions of the order.

342F   Orders under section 339 or 340 in pension-sharing cases: supplementary

(1) On the transferor's trustee in bankruptcy making a written request to the person responsible for the destination arrangement, that person shall provide the trustee with such information about—

(a) the arrangement,

(b) the transferee's rights under it, and

(c) where the destination arrangement is the shared arrangement, the transferor's rights under it,

as the trustee may reasonably require for, or in connection with, the making of applications under sections 339 and 340.

(2) Where the shared arrangement is not the destination arrangement, the person responsible for the shared arrangement shall, on the transferor's trustee in bankruptcy making a written request to that person, provide the trustee with such information about—

(a) the arrangement, and

(b) the transferor's rights under it,

as the trustee may reasonably require for, or in connection with, the making of applications under sections 339 and 340.

(3) On the transferor's trustee in bankruptcy making a written request to the person responsible for any intermediate arrangement, that person shall provide the trustee with such information about—

(a) the arrangement, and

(b) the transferee's rights under it,

as the trustee may reasonably require for, or in connection with, the making of applications under sections 339 and 340.

(4) In subsection (3) "intermediate arrangement" means a pension arrangement, other than the shared arrangement or the destination

arrangement, in relation to which the following conditions are fulfilled—

  (a) there was a time when the transferee had rights under the arrangement that were derived (directly or indirectly) from the pension-sharing transaction, and

  (b) the transferee's rights under the destination arrangement (so far as derived from the pension-sharing transaction) are to any extent derived (directly or indirectly) from the rights mentioned in paragraph (a).

(5) Nothing in—

  (a) any provision of section 159 of the Pension Schemes Act 1993 or section 91 of the Pensions Act 1995 (which prevent assignment and the making of orders which restrain a person from receiving anything which he is prevented from assigning),

  (b) any provision of any enactment (whether passed or made before or after the passing of the Welfare Reform and Pensions Act 1999) corrresponding to any of the provisions mentioned in paragraph (a), or

  (c) any provision of the destination arrangement corresponding to any of those provisions,

applies to a court exercising its powers under section 339 or 340.

(6) Regulations may, for the purposes of sections 339 to 342, sections 342D and 342E and this section, make provision about the calculation and verification of—

  (a) any such value as is mentioned in section 342E(4)(c);

  (b) any such amounts as are mentioned in section 342E(6)(a) and (b).

(7) The power conferred by subsection (6) includes power to provide for calculation or verification—

  (a) in such manner as may, in the particular case, be approved by a prescribed person; or

  (b) in accordance with guidance—

    (i)   from time to time prepared by a prescribed person, and

    (ii) approved by the Secretary of State.

(8) In section 342E and this section, references to the person responsible for a pension arrangement are to—

(a)   the trustees, managers or provider of the arrangement, or

(b)   the person having functions in relation to the arrangement corresponding to those of a trustee, manager or provider.

(9) In this section—

"prescribed" means prescribed by regulations;

"regulations" means regulations made by the Secretary of State.

(10) Regulations under this section may—

(a)   make different provision for different cases;

(b)   contain such incidental, supplemental and transitional provisions as appear to the Secretary of State necessary or expedient.

(11) Regulations under this section shall be made by statutory instrument subject to annulment in pursuance of a resolution of either House of Parliament.'

72. In section 384(1) (meaning of 'prescribed' in the second Group of Parts), after 'Subject to the next subsection' insert 'and sections 342C(7) and 342F(9) in Chapter V of Part IX'.

Income and Corporation Taxes Act 1988 (c 1)

73. The Income and Corporation Taxes Act 1988 is amended as follows.

74. In section 172(3) (exceptions from tax), for 'earnings threshold' substitute 'secondary threshold'.

75. In section 617(2) (social security benefits and contributions), after paragraph (ae) insert—

'(af) payments made under regulations under section 79 of the Welfare Reform and Pensions Act 1999 or under any corresponding enactment having effect with respect to Northern Ireland;'.

Social Security Contributions and Benefits Act 1992 (c 4)

76. The Contributions and Benefits Act has effect subject to the following amendments.

77.—(1) Section 122(1) (interpretation of Parts I to VI etc.) is amended as follows.

(2) In the definition of 'current', after 'limits' insert 'and primary and secondary thresholds'.

(3) In the definition beginning with 'lower earnings limit'—

    (a) for 'and "earnings threshold"' substitute '"primary threshold" and "secondary threshold"'; and

    (b) for 'the earnings' substitute 'the primary or secondary'.

78.—(1) Paragraph 1 of Schedule 1 (supplementary provisions relating to contributions) is amended in accordance with sub-paragraphs (2) to (5).

(2) For 'earnings threshold' (wherever occurring) substitute 'secondary threshold'.

(3) For 'lower earnings limit' (wherever occurring) substitute 'primary threshold'.

(4) Omit sub-paragraphs (4) and (5).

(5) After sub-paragraph (9) add—

    '(10) In relation to earners paid otherwise than weekly, any reference in this paragraph to—

    (a) the primary or the secondary threshold, or

    (b) the upper earnings limit,

    shall be construed as a reference to the equivalent of that threshold or limit prescribed under section 5(4) above.'

(6) In paragraph 6 of that Schedule—

    (a) in sub-paragraph (5), for 'section 159A' substitute 'section 4A, 159A'; and

    (b) in sub-paragraph (6), after 'relating' insert 'to relevant payments or benefits within the meaning of section 4A above or (as the case may be)'.

Social Security Administration Act 1992 (c 5)

79. The Administration Act has effect subject to the following amendments.

80. After section 140E insert—

'140EE   Financing of other expenditure

(1) The Secretary of State may make to a local authority such payments as he thinks fit in respect of expenses incurred by the authority in connection with the carrying out of any relevant function—

    (a) by the authority,

    (b) by any person providing services to the authority, or

    (c) by any person authorised by the authority to carry out that function.

(2) In subsection (1) "relevant function" means any function conferred by virtue of section 2A, 2C or 7A above.

(3) The following provisions, namely—

    (a) in section 140B, subsections (1), (3), (4), (5)(b), (7)(b) and (8), and

    (b) section 140C,

apply in relation to a payment under this section as in relation to a payment of subsidy.

(4) The Secretary of State may (without prejudice to the generality of his powers in relation to the amount of subsidy) take into account the fact that an amount has been paid under this section in respect of costs falling within section 140B(4A)(a) above.'

81. In section 170(5) (enactments conferring functions in respect of which Social Security Advisory Committee is to advise)—

    (a) in the definition of 'the relevant enactments', after paragraph (ad) insert—

        '(ae) sections 60, 72 and 79 of the Welfare Reform and Pensions Act 1999;'; and

    (b) in the definition of 'the relevant Northern Ireland enactments', after paragraph (ad) insert—

        '(ae) any provisions in Northern Ireland which correspond to sections 60, 72 and 79 of the Welfare Reform and Pensions Act 1999;'.

82. In section 189 (regulations and orders—general), after subsection (7) insert—

    '(7A) Without prejudice to the generality of any of the preceding provisions of this section, regulations under any of sections 2A to 2C and 7A above may provide for all or any of the provisions of the regulations to apply only in relation to any area or areas specified in the regulations.'

83. In section 190 (Parliamentary control of orders and regulations), in subsection (1) (instruments subject to the affirmative procedure), before the 'or' at the end of paragraph (a) insert—

'(aa) the first regulations to be made under section 2A;'.

Social Security Contributions and Benefits (Northern Ireland) Act 1992 (c 7)

84. The Social Security Contributions and Benefits (Northern Ireland) Act 1992 has effect subject to the following amendments.

85.—(1) Section 121(1) (interpretation of Parts I to VI etc.) is amended as follows.

(2) In the definition of 'current', after 'limits' insert 'and primary and secondary thresholds'.

(3) In the definition beginning with 'lower earnings limit'—

(a) for 'and "earnings threshold"' substitute ' "primary threshold" and "secondary threshold"'; and
(b) for 'the earnings' substitute 'the primary or secondary'.

86.—(1) Paragraph 1 of Schedule 1 (supplementary provisions relating to contributions) is amended in accordance with sub-paragraphs (2) to (5).

(2) For 'earnings threshold' (wherever occurring) substitute 'secondary threshold'.

(3) For 'lower earnings limit' (wherever occurring) substitute 'primary threshold'.

(4) Omit sub-paragraphs (4) and (5).

(5) After sub-paragraph (9) add—

'(10) In relation to earners paid otherwise than weekly, any reference in this paragraph to—

(a) the primary or the secondary threshold, or
(b) the upper earnings limit,

shall be construed as a reference to the equivalent of that threshold or limit prescribed under section 5(4) above.'

(6) In paragraph 6 of that Schedule—

    (a) in sub-paragraph (5), for 'section 155A' substitute 'section 4A, 155A'; and

    (b) in sub-paragraph (6), after 'relating' insert 'to relevant payments or benefits within the meaning of section 4A above or (as the case may be)'.

Social Security Act 1998 (c 14)

87. In Schedule 2 to the Social Security Act 1998 (decisions against which no appeal lies), after paragraph 5 insert—

'Work-focused interviews

5A. A decision terminating or reducing the amount of a person's benefit made in consequence of any decision made under regulations under section 2A of the Administration Act (work-focused interviews).'

Matrimonial Causes Act 1973
Parts II and IV

(as amended by the Welfare Reform and Pensions Act 1999)

ARRANGEMENT OF SECTIONS

. . .

PART II

FINANCIAL RELIEF FOR PARTIES TO MARRIAGE AND CHILDREN OF FAMILY

. . .

PART IV

MISCELLANEOUS AND SUPPLEMENTAL

. . .

An Act to consolidate certain enactments relating to matrimonial proceedings, maintenance agreements, and declarations of legitimacy, validity of marriage and British nationality, with amendments to give effect to recommendations of the Law Commission.   [23 May 1973]

. . .

PART II

FINANCIAL RELIEF FOR PARTIES TO MARRIAGE AND CHILDREN OF FAMILY

Financial provision and property adjustment orders

21   Financial provision and property adjustment orders

(1) The financial provision orders for the purposes of this Act are the orders for periodical or lump sum provision available (subject to the provisions of this Act) under section 23 below for the purpose of adjusting the financial position of the parties to a marriage and any children of the family in connection with proceedings for divorce, nullity of marriage or judicial separation and under section 27(6) below on proof of neglect by one party to a marriage to provide, or to make a proper contribution towards, reasonable maintenance for the other or a child of the family, that is to say—

(a) any order for periodical payments in favour of a party to a marriage under section 23(1)(a) or 27(6)(a) or in favour of a child of the family under section 23(1)(d), (2) or (4) or 27(6)(d);

(b) any order for secured periodical payments in favour of a party to a marriage under section 23(1)(b) or 27(6)(b) or in favour of a child of the family under section 23(1)(e), (2) or (4) or 27(6)(e); and

(c) any order for lump sum provision in favour of a party to a marriage under section 23(1)(c) or 27(6)(c) or in favour of a child of the family under section 23(1)(f), (2) or (4) or 27(6)(f);

and references in this Act (except in paragraphs 17(1) and 23 of Schedule 1 below) to periodical payments orders, secured periodical payments orders, and orders for the payment of a lump sum are references to all or some of the financial provision orders requiring the sort of financial provision in question according as the context of each reference may require.

(2) The property adjustment orders for the purposes of this Act are the orders dealing with property rights available (subject to the provisions of this Act) under section 24 below for the purpose of adjusting the financial position of the parties to a marriage and any children of the family on or after the grant of a decree of divorce, nullity of marriage or judicial separation, that is to say—

(a) any order under subsection (1)(a) of that section for a transfer of property;

(b) any order under subsection (1)(b) of that section for a settlement of property; and

(c) any order under subsection (1)(c) or (d) of that section for a variation of settlement.

21A   Pension sharing orders

(1) For the purposes of this Act, a pension sharing order is an order which—

(a) provides that one party's—
  (i) shareable rights under a specified pension arrangement, or
  (ii) shareable state scheme rights,
  be subject to pension sharing for the benefit of the other party, and
(b) specifies the percentage value to be transferred.

(2) In subsection (1) above—

(a) the reference to shareable rights under a pension arrangement is to rights in relation to which pension sharing is available under Chapter I of Part IV of the Welfare Reform and Pensions Act 1999, or under corresponding Northern Ireland legislation,

(b) the reference to shareable state scheme rights is to rights in relation to which pension sharing is available under Chapter II of Part IV of the Welfare Reform and Pensions Act 1999, or under corresponding Northern Ireland legislation, and

(c) "party" means a party to a marriage.

Amendments—Welfare Reform and Pensions Act 1999, s 19, Sch 3.

Ancillary relief in connection with divorce proceedings etc

22 Maintenance pending suit

On a petition for divorce, nullity of marriage or judicial separation, the court may make an order for maintenance pending suit, that is to say, an order requiring either party to the marriage to make to the other such periodical payments for his or her maintenance and for such term, being a term beginning not earlier than the date of the presentation of the petition and ending with the date of the determination of the suit, as the court thinks reasonable.

23 Financial provision orders in connection with divorce proceedings etc

(1) On granting a decree of divorce, a decree of nullity of marriage or a decree of judicial separation or at any time thereafter (whether, in the case of a decree of divorce or of nullity of marriage, before or after the decree is made absolute), the court may make any one or more of the following orders, that is to say—

(a) an order that either party to the marriage shall make to the other such periodical payments, for such term, as may be specifed in the order;

(b) an order that either party to the marriage shall secure to the other to the satisfaction of the court such periodical payments, for such term, as may be so specified;

(c) an order that either party to the marriage shall pay to the other such lump sum or sums as may be so specified;

(d) an order that a party to the marriage shall make to such person as may be specified in the order for the benefit of a child of the family, or to such a child, such periodical payments, for such term, as may be so specified;

(e) an order that a party to the marriage shall secure to such person as may be so specified for the benefit of such a child, or to such a child, to the satisfaction of the court, such periodical payments, for such term, as may be so specified;

(f) an order that a party to the marriage shall pay to such person as may be so specified for the benefit of such a child, or to such a child, such lump sum as may be so specified;

subject, however, in the case of an order under paragraph (d), (e) or (f) above, to the restrictions imposed by section 29(1) and (3) below on the making of financial provision orders in favour of children who have attained the age of eighteen.

(2) The court may also, subject to those restrictions, make any one or more of the orders mentioned in subsection (1)(d), (e) and (f) above—

(a) in any proceedings for divorce, nullity of marriage or judicial separation, before granting a decree; and

(b) where any such proceedings are dismissed after the beginning of the trial, either forthwith or within a reasonable period after the dismissal.

(3) Without prejudice to the generality of subsection (1)(c) or (f) above—

(a) an order under this section that a party to a marriage shall pay a lump sum to the other party may be made for the purpose of enabling that other party to meet any liabilities or expenses reasonably incurred by him or her in maintaining himself or herself or any child of the family before making an application for an order under this section in his or her favour;

(b) an order under this section for the payment of a lump sum to or for the benefit of a child of the family may be made for the purpose of enabling any liabilities or expenses reasonably incurred by or for the benefit of that child before the making of an application for an order under this section in his favour to be met; and

(c) an order under this section for the payment of a lump sum may provide for the payment of that sum by instalments of such amount as may be specified in the order and may require the payment of the instalments to be secured to the satisfaction of the court.

(4) The power of the court under subsection (1) or (2)(a) above to make an order in favour of a child of the family shall be exercisable from time to time; and where the court makes an order in favour of a child under subsection (2)(b) above, it may from time to time, subject to the restrictions mentioned in subsection (1) above, make a further order in his favour of any of the kinds mentioned in subsection (1)(d), (e) or (f) above.

(5) Without prejudice to the power to give a direction under section 30 below for the settlement of an instrument by conveyancing counsel, where an order is made under subsection (1)(a), (b) or (c) above on or after granting a decree of divorce or nullity of marriage, neither the order nor any settlement made in pursuance of the order shall take effect unless the decree has been made absolute.

(6) Where the court—

(a) makes an order under this section for the payment of a lump sum; and

(b) directs—

    (i) that payment of that sum or any part of it shall be deferred; or

    (ii) that the sum or any part of it shall be paid by instalments,

the court may order that the amount deferred or the instalments shall carry interest at such rate as may be specified by the order from such date, not earlier than the date of the order, as may be so specified, until the date when payment of it is due.

Amendments—Administration of Justice Act 1982, s 16.

24 Property adjustment orders in connection with divorce proceedings etc

(1) On granting a decree of divorce, a decree of nullity of marriage or a decree of judicial separation or at any time thereafter (whether, in the case of a decree of divorce or of nullity of marriage, before or after the decree is made absolute), the court may make any one or more of the following orders, that is to say—

(a) an order that a party to the marriage shall transfer to the other party, to any child of the family or to such person as may be specified in the order for the benefit of such a child such property as may be so specified, being property to which the first-mentioned party is entitled, either in possession or reversion;

(b)   an order that a settlement of such property as may be so specified, being property to which a party to the marriage is so entitled, be made to the satisfaction of the court for the benefit of the other party to the marriage and of the children of the family or either or any of them;

(c)   an order varying for the benefit of the parties to the marriage and of the children of the family or either or any of them any ante-nuptial or post-nuptial settlement (including such a settlement made by will or codicil) made on the parties to the marriage, other than one in the form of a pension arrangement (within the meaning of section 25D below);

(d)   an order extinguishing or reducing the interest of either of the parties to the marriage under any such settlement, other than one in the form of a pension arrangement (within the meaning of section 25D below);

subject, however, in the case of an order under paragraph (a) above, to the restrictions imposed by section 29(1) and (3) below on the making of orders for a transfer of property in favour of children who have attained the age of eighteen.

(2) The court may make an order under subsection (1)(c) above notwithstanding that there are no children of the family.

(3) Without prejudice to the power to give a direction under section 30 below for the settlement of an instrument by conveyancing counsel, where an order is made under this section on or after granting a decree of divorce or nullity of marriage, neither the order nor any settlement made in pursuance of the order shall take effect unless the decree has been made absolute.

Amendments—Welfare Reform and Pensions Act 1999, s 19, Sch 3.

24A   Orders for sale of property

(1) Where the court makes under section 23 or 24 of this Act a secured periodical payments order, an order for the payment of a lump sum or a property adjustment order, then, on making that order or at any time thereafter, the court may make a further order for the sale of such property as may be specified in the order, being property in which or in the proceeds of sale of which either or both of the parties to the marriage has or have a beneficial interest, either in possession or reversion.

(2) Any order made under subsection (1) above may contain such consequential or supplementary provisions as the court thinks fit and, without prejudice to the generality of the foregoing provision, may include—

(a) provision requiring the making of a payment out of the proceeds of sale of the property to which the order relates, and

(b) provision requiring any such property to be offered for sale to a person, or class of persons, specified in the order.

(30 Where an order is made under subsection (1) above on or after the grant of a decree of divorce or nullity of marriage, the order shall not take effect unless the decree has been made absolute.

(4) Where an order is made under subsection (1) above, the court may direct that the order, or such provision thereof as the court may specify, shall not take effect until the occurrence of an event specified by the court or the expiration of a period so specified.

(5) Where an order under subsection (1) above contains a provision requiring the proceeds of sale of the property to which the order relates to be used to secure periodical payments to a party to the marriage, the order shall cease to have effect on the death or re-marriage of that person.

(6) Where a party to a marriage has a beneficial interest in any property, or in the proceeds of sale thereof, and some other person who is not a party to the marriage also has a beneficial interest in that property or in the proceeds of sale thereof, then, before deciding whether to make an order under this section in relation to that property, it shall be the duty of the court to give that other person an opportunity to make representations with respect to the order; and any representations made by that other person shall be included among the circumstances to which the court is required to have regard under section 25(1) below.

Amendments—Matrimonial Homes and Property Act 1981, s 7; Matrimonial and Family Proceedings Act 1984, s 46(1), Sch 1, para 11; Welfare Reform and Pensions Act 1999, s 19, Sch 3.

24B Pension sharing orders in connection with divorce proceedings etc

(1) On granting a decree of divorce or a decree of nullity of marriage or at any time thereafter (whether before or after the decree is made absolute), the court may, on an application made under this section, make one or more pension sharing orders in relation to the marriage.

(2) A pension sharing order under this section is not to take effect unless the decree on or after which it is made has been made absolute.

(3) A pension sharing order under this section may not be made in relation to a pension arrangement which—

(a)   is the subject of a pension sharing order in relation to the marriage, or

(b)   has been the subject of pension sharing between the parties to the marriage.

(4) A pension sharing order under this section may not be made in relation to shareable state scheme rights if—

(a)   such rights are the subject of a pension sharing order in relation to the marriage, or

(b)   such rights have been the subject of pension sharing between the parties to the marriage.

(5) A pension sharing order under this section may not be made in relation to the rights of a person under a pension arrangement if there is in force a requirement imposed by virtue of section 25B or 25C below which relates to benefits or future benefits to which he is entitled under the pension arrangement.

Amendments—Welfare Reform and Pensions Act 1999, s 19, Sch 3.

24C   Pension sharing orders: duty to stay

(1) No pension sharing order may be made so as to take effect before the end of such period after the making of the order as may be prescribed by regulations made by the Lord Chancellor.

(2) The power to make regulations under this section shall be exercisable by statutory instrument which shall be subject to annulment in pursuance of a resolution of either House of Parliament.

Amendments—Welfare Reform and Pensions Act 1999, s 19, Sch 3.

24D   Pension sharing orders: apportionment of charges

If a pension sharing order relates to rights under a pension arrangement, the court may include in the order provision about the apportionment between the parties of any charge under section 41 of the Welfare Reform and Pensions Act 1999 (charges in respect of pension sharing costs), or under corresponding Northern Ireland legislation.

Amendments—Welfare Reform and Pensions Act 1999, s 19, Sch 3.

25   Matters to which court is to have regard in deciding how to exercise its powers under ss 23, 24 and 24A

(1) It shall be the duty of the court in deciding whether to exercise its powers under section 23, 24, 24A or 24B above and, if so, in what manner, to have regard to all the circumstances of the case, first consideration being given to the welfare while a minor of any child of the family who has not attained the age of eighteen.

(2) As regards the exercise of the powers of the court under section 23(1)(a), (b) or (c), 24, 24A or 24B above in relation to a party to the marriage, the court shall in particular have regard to the following matters—

(a) the income, earning capacity, property and other financial resources which each of the parties to the marriage has or is likely to have in the foreseeable future, including in the case of earning capacity any increase in that capacity which it would in the opinion of the court be reasonable to expect a party to the marriage to take steps to acquire;

(b) the financial needs, obligations and responsibilities which each of the parties to the marriage has or is likely to have in the foreseeable future;

(c) the standard of living enjoyed by the family before the breakdown of the marriage;

(d) the age of each party to the marriage and the duration of the marriage;

(e) any physical or mental disability of either of the parties to the marriage;

(f) the contributions which each of the parties has made or is likely in the foreseeable future to make to the welfare of the family, including any contribution by looking after the home or caring for the family;

(g) the conduct of each of the parties, if that conduct is such that it would in the opinion of the court be inequitable to disregard it;

(h) in the case of proceedings for divorce or nullity of marriage, the value to each of the parties to the marriage of any benefit which, by reason of the dissolution or annulment of the marriage, that party will lose the chance of acquiring.

(3) As regards the exercise of the powers of the court under section 23(1)(d), (e) or (f), (2) or (4), 24 or 24A above in relation to a child of the family, the court shall in particular have regard to the following matters—

   (a)   the financial needs of the child;
   (b)   the income, earning capacity (if any), property and other financial resources of the child;
   (c)   any physical or mental disability of the child;
   (d)   the manner in which he was being and in which the parties to the marriage expected him to be educated or trained;
   (e)   the considerations mentioned in relation to the parties to the marriage in paragraphs (a), (b), (c) and (e) of subsection (2) above.

(4) As regards the exercise of the powers of the court under section 23(1)(d), (e) or (f), (2) or (4), 24 or 24A above against a party to a marriage in favour of a child of the family who is not the child of that party, the court shall also have regard—

   (a)   to whether that party assumed any responsibility for the child's maintenance, and, if so, to the extent to which, and the basis upon which, that party assumed such responsibility and to the length of time for which that party discharged such responsibility;
   (b)   to whether in assuming and discharging such responsibility that party did so knowing that the child was not his or her own;
   (c)   to the liability of any other person to maintain the child.

Amendments—Matrimonial and Family Proceedings Act 1984, s 3; Pensions Act 1995, s 166; Welfare Reform and Pensions Act 1999, s 19, Sch 3.

25A   Exercise of court's powers in favour of party to marriage on decree of divorce or nullity of marriage

(1) Where on or after the grant of a decree of divorce or nullity of marriage the court decides to exercise its powers under section 23(1)(a), (b) or (c), 24, 24A or 24B above in favour of a party to the marriage, it shall be the duty of the court to consider whether it would be appropriate so to exercise those powers that the financial obligations of each party towards the other will be terminated as soon after the grant of the decree as the court considers just and reasonable.

(2) Where the court decides in such a case to make a periodical payments or secured periodical payments order in favour of a party to the marriage, the court shall in particular consider whether it would be appropriate to require

those payments to be made or secured only for such term as would in the opinion of the court be sufficient to enable the party in whose favour the order is made to adjust without undue hardship to the termination of his or her financial dependence on the other party.

(3) Where on or after the grant of a decree of divorce or nullity of marriage an application is made by a party to the marriage for a periodical payments or secured periodical payments order in his or her favour, then, if the court considers that no continuing obligation should be imposed on either party to make or secure periodical payments in favour of the other, the court may dismiss the application with a direction that the applicant shall not be entitled to make any future application in relation to that marriage for an order under section 23(1)(a) or (b) above.

Amendments—Inserted by Matrimonial and Family Proceedings Act 1984, s 3; Welfare Reform and Pensions Act 1999, s 19, Sch 3.

25B   Pensions

(1) The matters to which the court is to have regard under section 25(2) above include—

(a)   in the case of paragraph (a), any benefits under a pension arrangement which a party to the marriage has or is likely to have, and

(b)   in the case of paragraph (h), any benefits under a pension arrangement which, by reason of the dissolution or annulment of the marriage, a party to the marriage will lose the chance of acquiring,

and, accordingly, in relation to benefits under a pension arrangement, section 25(2)(a) above shall have effect as if 'in the foreseeable future' were omitted.

(2) (*repealed*)

(3) The following provisions apply where, having regard to any benefits under a pension arrangement, the court determines to make an order under section 23 above.

(4) To the extent to which the order is made having regard to any benefits under a pension arrangement, the order may require the

person responsible for the pension arrangement in question, if at any time any payment in respect of any benefits under the arrangement becomes due to the party with pension rights, to make a payment for the benefit of the other party.

(5) The order must express the amount of any payment required to be made by virtue of subsection (4) above as a percentage of the payment which becomes due to the party with pension rights.

(6) Any such payment by the person responsible for the arrangement—

(a) shall discharge so much of his liability to the party with pension rights as corresponds to the amount of the payment, and

(b) shall be treated for all purposes as a payment made by the party with pension rights in or towards the discharge of his liability under the order.

(7) Where the party with pension rights has a right of commutation under the arrangement, the order may require him to exercise it to any extent; and this section applies to any payment due in consequence of commutation in pursuance of the order as it applies to other payments in respect of benefits under the arrangement.

(7A) The power conferred by subsection (7) above may not be exercised for the purpose of commuting a benefit payable to the party with pension rights to a benefit payable to the other party.

(7B) The power conferred by subsection (4) or (7) above may not be exercised in relation to a pension arrangement which—

(a) is the subject of a pension sharing order in relation to the marriage, or

(b) has been the subject of pension sharing between the parties to the marriage.

(7C) In subsection (1) above, references to benefits under a pension arrangement include any benefits by way of pension, whether under a pension arrangement or not.

Amendments—Pensions Act 1995, s 166; Welfare Reform and Pensions Act 1999, s 21, Sch 4.

25C Pensions: lump sums

(1) The power of the court under section 23 above to order a party to a marriage to pay a lump sum to the other party includes, where the benefits which the party with pension rights has or is likely to have under a pension arrangement include any lump sum payable in respect of his death, power to make any of the following provision by the order.

(2) The court may—

  (a) if the person responsible for the pensions arrangement in question has power to determine the person to whom the sum, or any part of it, is to be paid, require him to pay the whole or part of that sum, when it becomes due, to the other party,

  (b) if the party with pension rights has power to nominate the person to whom the sum, or any part of it, is to be paid, require the party with pension rights to nominate the other party in respect of the whole or part of that sum,

  (c) in any other case, require the person responsible for the pension arrangement in question to pay the whole or part of that sum, when it becomes due, for the benefit of the other party instead of to the person to whom, apart from the order, it would be paid.

(3) Any payment by the person responsible for the arrangement under an order made under section 23 above by virtue of this section shall discharge so much of his liability in respect of the party with pension rights as corresponds to the amount of the payment.

(4) The powers conferred by this section may not be exercised in relation to a pension arrangement which—

  (a) is the subject of a pension sharing order in relation to the marriage, or

  (b) has been the subject of pension sharing between the parties to the marriage.

Amendments—Inserted by Pensions Act 1995, s 166; Welfare Reform and Pensions Act 1999, s 21, Sch 4.

25D   Pensions: supplementary

(1) Where—

   (a)   an order made under section 23 above by virtue of section 25B or
         25C above imposes any requirement on the person responsible for a
         pension arrangement ('the first arrangement') and the party with
         pension rights acquires rights under another pension arrangement
         ('the new arrangement') which are derived (directly or indirectly)
         from the whole of his rights under the first arrangement, and
   (b)   the person responsible for the new arrangement has been given
         notice in accordance with regulations made by the Lord Chancellor,

the order shall have effect as if it had been made instead of respect of the
person responsible for the new arrangement.

(2) The Lord Chancellor may by Regulations—

   (a)   in relation to any provision of sctions 25B or 25C above which
         authorises the court making an order under section 23 above to
         require the person responsible for a pension arrangement to make a
         payment for the benefit of the other party, make provision as to the
         person to whom, and the terms on which, the payment is to be made,
   (ab) make, in relation to payment under a mistaken belief as to the
         continuation in force of a provision included by virtue of section 25B
         or 25C above in an order under section 23 above, provision about the
         rights or liabilities of the payer, the payee or the person to whom the
         payment was due,
   (b)   require notices to be given in respect of changes of circumstances
         relevant to such orders which include provision made by virtue of
         sections 25B and 25C above,
   (ba) make provision for the person responsible for a pension arrange-
         ment to be discharged in prescribed circumstances from a require-
         ment imposed by virtue of section 25B or 25C above,
   (e)   make provision about calculation and verification in relation to the
         valuation of—
         (i)   benefits under a pension arrangement, or
         (ii)   shareable state scheme rights,
         for the purposes of the court's functions in connection with the
         exercise of any of its powers under this Part of this Act.

(2A) Regulations under subsection (2)(e) above may include—

(a) provision for calculation or verification in accordance with guidance from time to time prepared by a prescribed person, and

(b) provision by reference to regulations under section 30 or 49(4) of the Welfare Reform and Pensions Act 1999.

(2B) Regulations under subsection (2) above may make different provision for different cases.

(2C) Power to make regulations under this section shall be exercisable by statutory instrument which shall be subject to annulment in pursuance of a resolution of either House of Parliament.

(3) In this section and sections 25B and 25C above—

'occupational pension scheme' has the same meaning as in the Pension Schemes Act 1993;

'the party with pension rights' means the party to the marriage who has or is likely to have benefits under a pension arrangement and 'the other party' means the other party to the marriage;

'pension arrangement' means—

(a) an occupational pension scheme,

(b) a personal pension scheme,

(c) a retirement annuity contract,

(d) an annuity or insurance policy purchased, or transferred, for the purpose of giving effect to rights under an occupational pension scheme or a personal pension scheme, and

(e) an annuity purchased, or entered into, for the purpose of discharging liability in respect of a pension credit under section 29(1)(b) of the Welfare Reform and Pensions Act 1999 or under corresponding Northern Ireland legislation;

'personal pension scheme' has the same meaning as in the Pension Schemes Act 1993;

'prescribed' means prescribed by regulations;

'retirement annuity contract' means a contract or scheme approved under Chapter III of Part XIV of the Income and Corporation Taxes Act 1988;

'shareable state scheme rights' has the same meaning as in section 21A(1) above; and 'trustees or managers', in relation to an occupation pension scheme or a personal pension scheme, means—

(a) in the case of a scheme established under a trust, the trustees of the scheme, and

(b) in any other case, the managers of the scheme.

(4) In this section and sections 25B and 25C above, references to the person responsible for a pension arrangement are—

(a) in the case of an occupational pension scheme or a personal pension scheme, to the trustees or managers of the scheme,

(b) in the case of a retirement annuity contract or an annuity falling within paragraph (d) or (e) of the definition of 'pension arrangement' above, the provider of the annuity, and

(c) in the case of an insurance policy falling within paragraph (d) of the definition of that expression, the insurer.

Amendments—Pensions Act 1995, s 166; Welfare Reform and Pensions Act 1999, s 21, Sch 4.

26   Commencement of proceedings for ancillary relief etc

(1) Where a petition for divorce, nullity of marriage or judicial separation has been presented, then, subject to subsection (2) below, proceedings for maintenance pending suit under section 22 above, for a financial provision order under section 23 above, or for a property adjustment order may be begun, subject to and in accordance with rules of court, at any time after the presentation of the petition.

(2) Rules of court may provide, in such cases as may be prescribed by the rules—

(a) that applications for any such relief as is mentioned in subsection (1) above shall be made in the petition or answer; and

(b) that applications for any such relief which are not so made, or are not made until after the expiration of such period following the presentation of the petition or filing of the answer as may be so prescribed, shall be made only with the leave of the court.

Financial provison in case of neglect to maintain

27 Financial provision orders etc in case of neglect by party to marriage to maintain other party or child of the family

(1) Either party to a marriage may apply to the court for an order under this section on the ground that the other party to the marriage (in this section referred to as the respondent)—

  (a) has failed to provide reasonable maintenance for the applicant, or
  (b) has failed to provide, or to make a proper contribution towards, reasonable maintenance for any child of the family.

(2) The court shall not entertain an application under this section unless—

  (a) the applicant or the respondent is domiciled in England and Wales on the date of the application; or
  (b) the applicant has been habitually resident there throughout the period of one year ending with that date; or
  (c) the respondent is resident there on that date.

(3) Where an application under this section is made on the ground mentioned in subsection (1)(a) above, then, in deciding—

  (a) whether the respondent has failed to provide reasonable maintenance for the applicant, and
  (b) what order, if any, to make under this section in favour of the applicant,

the court shall have regard to all the circumstances of the case including the matters mentioned in section 25(2) above, and where an application is also made under this section in respect of a child of the family who has not attained the age of eighteen, first consideration shall be given to the welfare of the child while a minor.

(3A) Where an application under this section is made on the ground mentioned in subsection (1)(b) above then, in deciding—

  (a) whether the respondent has failed to provide, or to make a proper contribution towards, reasonable maintenance for the child of the family to whom the application relates, and
  (b) what order, if any, to make under this section in favour of the child,

the court shall have regard to all the circumstances of the case including the matters mentioned in section 25(3)(a) to (e) above, and where the child of the family to whom the application relates is not the child of the respondent, including also the matters mentioned in section 25(4) above.

(3B) In relation to an application under this section on the ground mentioned in subsection (1)(a) above, section 25(2)(c) above shall have effect as if for the reference therein to the breakdown of the marriage there were substituted a reference to the failure to provide reasonable maintenance for the applicant, and in relation to an application under this section on the ground mentioned in subsection (1)(b) above, section 25(2)(c) above (as it applies by virtue of section 25(3)(e) above) shall have effect as if for the reference therein to the breakdown of the marriage there were substituted a reference to the failure to provide, or to make a proper contribution towards, reasonable maintenance for the child of the family to whom the application relates.

(4) (*repealed*)

(5) Where on an application under this section it appears to the court that the applicant or any child of the family to whom the application relates is in immediate need of financial assistance, but it is not yet possible to determine what order, if any, should be made on the application, the court may make an interim order for maintenance, that is to say, an order requiring the respondent to make to the applicant until the determination of the application such periodical payments as the court thinks reasonable.

(6) Where on an application under this section the applicant satisfies the court of any ground mentioned in subsection (1) above, the court may make any one or more of the following orders, that is to say—

(a) an order that the respondent shall make to the applicant such periodical payments, for such term, as may be specified in the order;

(b) an order that the respondent shall secure to the applicant, to the satisfaction of the court, such periodical payments, for such term, as may be so specified;

(c) an order that the respondent shall pay to the applicant such lump sum as may be so specified;

(d) an order that the respondent shall make to such person as may be specified in the order for the benefit of the child to whom the application relates, or to that child, such periodical payments, for such term, as may be so specified;

(e) an order that the respondent shall secure to such person as may be so specified for the benefit of that child, or to that child, to the satisfaction of the court, such periodical payments, for such term, as may be so specified;

(f)   an order that the respondent shall pay to such person as may be so specified for the benefit of that child, or to that child, such lump sum as may be so specified;

subject, however, in the case of an order under paragraph (d), (e) or (f) above, to the restrictions imposed by section 29(1) and (3) below on the making of financial provision orders in favour of children who have attained the age of eighteen.

(6A) An application for the variation under section 31 of this Act of a periodical payments order or secured periodical payments order made under this section in favour of a child may, if the child has attained the age of sixteen, be made by the child himself.

(6B) Where a periodical payments order made in favour of a child under this section ceases to have effect on the date on which the child attains the age of sixteen or at any time after that date but before or on the date on which he attains the age of eighteen, then, if at any time before he attains the age of twenty-one an application is made by the child for an order under this subsection, the court shall have power by order to revive the first-mentioned order from such date as the court may specify, not being earlier than the date of the making of the application, and to exercise its powers under section 31 of this Act in relation to any order so revived.

(7) Without prejudice to the generality of subsection (6)(c) or (f) above, an order under this section for the payment of a lump sum—

(a)   may be made for the purpose of enabling any liabilities or expenses reasonably incurred in maintaining the applicant or any child of the family to whom the application relates before the making of the application to be met;

(b)   may provide for the payment of that sum by instalments of such amount as may be specified in the order and may require the payment of the instalments to be secured to the satisfaction of the court.

(8) (*repealed*)

Amendments—Domicile and Matrimonial Proceedings Act 1973, s 6(1); Domestic Proceedings and Magistrates' Courts Act 1978, ss 63, 89(2)(b), Sch 3; Matrimonial and Family Proceedings Act 1984, ss 4, 46(1), Sch 1, para 12; Family Law Reform Act 1987, s 33(1), Sch 2, para 52.

Additional provisions with respect to financial provision and property adjustment
orders

28   Duration of continuing financial provision orders in favour of party to marriage, and effect of remarriage

(1) Subject in the case of an order made on or after the grant of a decree of a divorce or nullity of marriage to the provisions of sections 25A(2) above and 31(7) below, the term to be specified in a periodical payments or secured periodical payments order in favour of a party to a marriage shall be such term as the court thinks fit, except that the term shall not begin before or extend beyond the following limits, that is to say—

   (a)   in the case of a periodical payments order, the term shall begin not earlier than the date of the making of an application for the order, and shall be so defined as not to extend beyond the death of either of the parties to the marriage or, where the order is made on or after the grant of a decree of divorce or nullity of marriage, the remarriage of the party in whose favour the order is made; and

   (b)   in the case of a secured periodical payments order, the term shall begin not earlier than the date of the making of an application for the order, and shall be so defined as not to extend beyond the death or, where the order is made on or after the grant of such a decree, the remarriage of the party in whose favour the order is made.

(1A) Where a periodical payments or secured periodical payments order in favour of a party to a marriage is made on or after the grant of a decree of divorce or nullity of marriage, the court may direct that that party shall not be entitled to apply under section 31 below for the extension of the term specified in the order.

(2) Where a periodical payments or secured periodical payments order in favour of a party to a marriage is made otherwise than on or after the grant of a decree of divorce or nullity of marriage, and the marriage in question is subsequently dissolved or annulled but the order continues in force, the order shall, notwithstanding anything in it, cease to have effect on the remarriage of that party, except in relation to any arrears due under it on the date of the remarriage.

(3) If after the grant of a decree dissolving or annulling a marriage either party to that marriage remarries whether at any time before or after the commencement of this Act, that party shall not be entitled to apply, by reference to the grant of that decree, for a financial provision order in his or

her favour, or for a property adjustment order, against the other party to that marriage.

Amendments—Matrimonial and Family Proceedings Act 1984, s 5.

29 Duration of continuing financial provision orders in favour of children, and age limit on making certain orders in their favour

(1) Subject to subsection (3) below, no financial provision order and no order for a transfer of property under section 24(1)(a) above shall be made in favour of a child who has attained the age of eighteen.

(2) The term to be specified in a periodical payments or secured periodical payments order in favour of a child may begin with the date of the making of an application for the order in question or any later date or a date ascertained in accordance with subsection (5) or (6) but—

- (a) shall not in the first instance extend beyond the date of the birthday of the child next following his attaining the upper limit of the compulsory school age (that is to say, the age that is for the time being that limit by virtue of section 35 of the Education Act 1944 together with any Order in Council made under that section) unless the court considers that in the circumstances of the case the welfare of the child requires that it should extend to a later date; and
- (d) shall not in any event, subject to subsection (3) below, extend beyond the date of the child's eighteenth birthday.

(3) Subsection (1) above, and paragraph (b) of subsection (2), shall not apply in the case of a child, if it appears to the court that—

- (a) the child is, or will be, or if an order were made without complying with either or both of those provisions would be, receiving instruction at an educational establishment or undergoing training for a trade, profession or vocation, whether or not he is also, or will also be, in gainful employment; or
- (b) there are special circumstances which justify the making of an order without complying with either or both of those provisions.

(4) Any periodical payments order in favour of a child shall, notwithstanding anything in the order, cease to have effect on the death of the person liable to make payments under the order, except in relation to any arrears due under the order on the date of the death.

(5) Where—

(a) a maintenance assessment ('the current assessment') is in force with respect to a child; and

(b) an application is made under Part II of this Act for a periodical payments or secured periodical payments order in favour of that child—

(i) in accordance with section 8 of the Child Support Act 1991, and

(ii) before the end of the period of 6 months beginning with the making of the current assessment,

the term to be specified in any such order made on that application may be expressed to begin on, or at any time after, the earliest permitted date.

(6) For the purposes of subsection (5) above, 'the earliest permitted date' is whichever is the later of—

(a) the date 6 months before the application is made; or

(b) the date on which the current assessment took effect or, where successive maintenance assessments have been continuously in force with respect to a child, on which the first of those assessments took effect.

(7) Where—

(a) a maintenance assessment ceases to have effect or is cancelled by or under any provision of the Child Support Act 1991; and

(b) an application is made, before the end of the period of 6 months beginning with the relevant date, for a periodical payments or secured periodical payments order in favour of a child with respect to whom that maintenance assessment was in force immediately before it ceased to have effect or was cancelled,

the term to be specified in any such order made on that application may begin with the date on which that maintenance assessment ceased to have effect or, as the case may be, the date with effect from which it was cancelled, or any later date.

(8) In subsection (7)(b) above,—

(a) where the maintenance assessment ceased to have effect, the relevant date is the date on which it is so ceased; and

(b) where the maintenance assessment was cancelled, the relevant date is the later of—

(i) the date on which the person who cancelled it did so, and

(ii) the date from which the cancellation first had effect.

Amendments—Matrimonial and Family Proceedings Act 1984, s 5; SI 1993/623.

30   Direction for settlement of instrument for securing payments or effecting property adjustment

Where the court decides to make a financial provision order requiring any payments to be secured or a property adjustment order—

(a)   it may direct that the matter be referred to one of the conveyancing counsel of the court for him to settle a proper instrument to be executed by all necessary parties; and

(b)   where the order is to be made in proceedings for divorce, nullity of marriage or judicial separation it may, if it thinks fit, defer the grant of the decree in question until the instrument has been duly executed.

Variation, discharge and enforcement of certain orders etc

31   Variation, discharge etc of certain orders for financial relief

(1)   Where the court has made an order to which this section applies, then, subject to the provisions of this section and of section 28(1A) above, the court shall have power to vary or discharge the order or to suspend any provision thereof temporarily and to revive the operation of any provision so suspended.

(2)   This section applies to the following orders, that is to say—

(a)   any order for maintenance pending suit and any interim order for maintenance;

(b)   any periodical payments order;

(c)   any secured periodical payments order;

(d)   any order made by virtue of section 23(3)(c) or 27(7)(b) above (provision for payment of a lump sum by instalments);

(dd) any deferred order made by virtue of section 23(1)(c) (lump sums) which includes provision made by virtue of—

(i)   section 25B(4), or

(ii)   section 25C,

(provision in respect of pension rights);

(e)   any order for a settlement of property under section 24(1)(b) or for a variation of settlement under section 24(1)(c) or (d) above, being an order made on or after the grant of a decree of judicial separation;

(f)   any order made under section 24A(1) above for the sale of property;

(g)   a pension sharing order under section 24B above which is made at a time before the decree has been made absolute.

(2A) Where the court has made an order referred to in subsection (2)(a), (b) or (c) above, then, subject to the provisions of this section, the court shall have power to remit the payment of any arrears due under the order or of any part thereof.

(2B) Where the court has made an order referred to in subsection (2)(dd)(ii) above, this section shall cease to apply to the order on the death of either of the parties to the marriage.

(3)   The powers exercisable by the court under this section in relation to an order shall be exercisable also in relation to any instrument executed in pursuance of the order.

(4)   The court shall not exercise the powers conferred by this section in relation to an order for a settlement under section 24(1)(b) or for a variation of settlement under section 24(1)(c) or (d) above except on an application made in proceedings—

(a)   for the rescission of the decree of judicial separation by reference to which the order was made, or

(b)   for the dissolution of the marriage in question.

(4A) In relation to an order which falls within paragraph (g) of subsection (2) above ('the subsection (2) order')—

(a)   the powers conferred by this section may be exercised—

(i)   only on an application made before the subsection (2) order has or, but for paragraph (b) below, would have taken effect; and

(ii)   only if, at the time when the application is made, the decree has not been made absolute; and

(b)   an application made in accordance with paragraph (a) above prevents the subsection (2) order from taking effect before the application has been dealt with.

(4B) No variation of a pension sharing order shall be made so as to take effect before the decree is made absolute.

(4C) The variation of a pension sharing order prevents the order taking effect before the end of such period after the making of the variation as may be prescribed by regulations made by the Lord Chancellor.

(5) Subject to subsections (7A) to (7G) below and without prejudice to any power exercisable by virtue of subsection (2)(d), (dd), (e) or (g) above or otherwise than by virtue of this section, no property adjustment order or pension sharing order shall be made on an application for the variation of a periodical payments or secured periodical payments order made (whether in favour of a party to a marriage or in favour of a child of the family) under section 23 above, and no order for the payment of a lump sum shall be made on an application for the variation of a periodical payments or secured periodical payments order in favour of a party to a marriage (whether made under section 23 or under section 27 above).

(6) Where the person liable to make payments under a secured periodical payments order has died, an application under this section relating to that order (and to any order made under section 24A(1) above which requires the proceeds of sale of property to be used for securing those payments) may be made by the person entitled to payments under the periodical payments order or by the personal representatives of the deceased person, but no such application shall, except with the permission of the court, be made after the end of the period of six months from the date on which representation in regard to the estate of that person is first taken out.

(7) In exercising the powers conferred by this section the court shall have regard to all the circumstances of the case, first consideration being given to the welfare while a minor of any child of the family who has not attained the age of eighteen, and the circumstances of the case shall include any change in any of the matters to which the court was required to have regard when making the order to which the application relates, and—

(a) in the case of a periodical payments or secured periodical payments order made on or after the grant of a decree of divorce or nullity of marriage, the court shall consider whether in all the circumstances and after having regard to any such change it would be appropriate to vary the order so that payments under the order are required to be made or secured only for such further period as will in the opinion of the court be sufficient (in the light of any proposed exercise by the court, where the marriage has been dissolved, of its powers under subsection (7B) below) to enable the party in whose favour the order was made to adjust without undue hardship to the termination of those payments;

(b) in a case where the party against whom the order was made has died, the circumstances of the case shall also include the changed circumstances resulting from his or her death.

(7A) Subsection (7B) below applies where, after the dissolution of a marriage, the court—

   (a)   discharges a periodical payments order or secured periodical payments order made in favour of a party to the marriage; or

   (b)   varies such an order so that payments under the order are required to be made or secured only for such further period as is determined by the court.

(7B) The court has power, in addition to any power it has apart from this subsection, to make supplemental provision consisting of any of—

   (a)   an order for the payment of a lump sum in favour of a party to the marriage;

   (b)   one or more property adjustment orders in favour of a party to the marriage;

  (ba) one or more pension sharing orders;

   (c)   a direction that the party in whose favour the original order discharged or varied was made is not entitled to make any further application for—

      (i)   a periodical payments or secured periodical payments order, or

     (ii)   an extension of the period to which the original order is limited by any variation made by the court.

(7C) An order for the payment of a lump sum made under subsection (7B) above may—

   (a)   provide for the payment of that sum by instalments of such amount as may be specified in the order; and

   (b)   require the payment of the instalments to be secured to the satisfaction of the court.

(7D) Section 23(6) above applies where the court makes an order for the payment of a lump sum under subsection (7B) above as it applies where the court makes such an order under section 23 above.

(7E) If under subsection (7B) above the court makes more than one property adjustment order in favour of the same party to the marriage, each of those orders must fall within a different paragraph of section 21(2) above.

(7F) Sections 24A and 30 above apply where the court makes a property adjustment order under subsection (7B) above as they apply where it makes such an order under section 24 above.

(7G) Subsections (3) to (5) of section 24B above apply in relation to a pension sharing order under subsection (7B) above as they apply in relation to a pension sharing order under that section.

(8) The personal representatives of a deceased person against whom a secured periodical payments order was made shall not be liable for having distributed any part of the estate of the deceased after the expiration of the period of six months referred to in subsection (6) above on the ground that they ought to have taken into account the possibility that the court might permit an application under this section to be made after that period by the person entitled to payments under the order; but this subsection shall not prejudice any power to recover any part of the estate so distributed arising by virtue of the making of an order in pursuance of this section.

(9) In considering for the purposes of subsection (6) above the question when representation was first taken out, a grant limited to settled land or to trust property shall be left out of account and a grant limited to real estate or to personal estate shall be left out of account unless a grant limited to the remainder of the estate has previously been made or is made at the same time.

(10) Where the court, in exercise of its powers under this section, decides to vary or discharge a periodical payments or secured periodical payments order, then, subject to section 28(1) and (2) above, the court shall have power to direct that the variation or discharge shall not take effect until the expiration of such period as may be specified in the order.

(11) Where—

(a) a periodical payments or secured periodical payments order in favour of more than one child ('the order') is in force;

(b) the order requires payments specified in it to be made to or for the benefit of more than one child without apportioning those payments between them;

(c) a maintenance assessment ('the assessment') is made with respect to one or more, but not all, of the children with respect to whom those payments are to be made; and

(d) an application is made, before the end of the period of 6 months beginning with the date on which the assessment was made, for the variation or discharge of the order,

the court may, in exercise of its powers under this section to vary or discharge the order, direct that the variation or discharge shall take effect from the date on which the assessment took effect or any later date.

(12) Where—

   (a)   an order ('the child order') of a kind prescribed for the purposes of section 10(1) of the Child Support Act 1991 is affected by a maintenance assessment;

   (b)   on the date on which the child order became so affected there was in force a periodical payments or secured periodical payments order ('the spousal order') in favour of a party to a marriage having the care of the child in whose favour the child order was made; and

   (c)   an application is made, before the end of the period of 6 months beginning with the date on which the maintenance assessment was made, for the spousal order to be varied or discharged,

the court may, in exercise of its powers under this section to vary or discharge the spousal order, direct that the variation or discharge shall take effect from the date on which the child order became so affected or any later date.

(13) For the purposes of subsection (12) above, an order is affected if it ceases to have effect or is modified by or under section 10 of the Child Support Act 1991.

(14) Subsections (11) and (12) above are without prejudice to any other power of the court to direct that the variation of discharge of an order under this section shall take effect from a date earlier than that on which the order for variation or discharge was made.

(15) The power to make regulations under subsection (4C) above shall be exercisable by statutory instrument which shall be subject to annulment in pursuance of a resolution of either House of Parliament.

Amendments—Matrimonial Homes and Property Act 1981, s 8(2); Administration of Justice Act 1982, s 51; Matrimonial and Family Proceedings Act 1984, s 6; SI 1993/623; Pensions Act 1995, s 166; Family Law Act 1996, Sch 8, para 16(5)(a), (6)(b), (7) (as modified by SI 1998/2572); Welfare Reform and Pensions Act 1999, s 19, Sch 3.

32   Payment of certain arrears unenforceable without the leave of the court

(1) A person shall not be entitled to enforce through the High Court or any county court the payment of any arrears due under an order for maintenance pending suit, an interim order for maintenance or any financial provision order without the leave of that court if those arrears became due more than twelve months before proceedings to enforce the payment of them are begun.

(2) The court hearing an application for the grant of leave under this section may refuse leave, or may grant leave subject to such restrictions and conditions (including conditions as to the allowing of time for payment or the making of payment by instalments) as that court thinks proper, or may remit the payment of the arrears or of any part thereof.

(3) An application for the grant of leave under this section shall be made in such manner as may be prescribed by rules of court.

33　Orders for repayment in certain cases of sums paid under certain orders

(1) Where on an application made under this section in relation to an order to which this section applies it appears to the court that by reason of—

(a) a change in the circumstances of the person entitled to, or liable to make, payments under the order since the order was made, or

(b) the changed circumstances resulting from the death of the person so liable,

the amount received by the person entitled to payments under the order in respect of a period after those circumstances changed or after the death of the person liable to make payments under the order, as the case may be, exceeds the amount which the person so liable or his or her personal representatives should have been required to pay, the court may order the respondent to the application to pay to the applicant such sum, not exceeding the amount of the excess, as the court thinks just.

(2) This section applies to the following orders, that is to say—

(a) any order for maintenance pending suit and any interim order for maintenance;

(b) any periodical payments order; and

(c) any secured periodical payments order.

(3) An application under this section may be made by the person liable to make payments under an order to which this section applies or his or her personal representatives and may be made against the person entitled to payments under the order or her or his personal representatives.

(4) An application under this section may be made in proceedings in the High Court or a county court for—

(a) the variation or discharge of the order to which this section applies, or

(b) leave to enforce, or the enforcement of, the payment of arrears under that order;

but when not made in such proceedings shall be made to a county court, and accordingly references in this section to the court are references to the High Court or a county court, as the circumstances require.

(5) The jurisdiction conferred on a county court by this section shall be exercisable notwithstanding that by reason of the amount claimed in the application the jurisdiction would not but for this subsection be exercisable by a county court.

(6) An order under this section for the payment of any sum may provide for the payment of that sum by instalments of such amount as may be specified in the order.

Consent orders

33A Consent orders for financial provision on property adjustment

(1) Notwithstanding anything in the preceding provisions of this Part of this Act, on an application for a consent order for financial relief the court may, unless it has reason to think that there are other circumstances into which it ought to inquire, make an order in the terms agreed on the basis only of the prescribed information furnished with the application.

(2) Subsection (1) above applies to an application for a consent order varying or discharging an order for financial relief as it applies to an application for an order for financial relief.

(3) In this section—

'consent order', in relation to an application for an order, means an order in the terms applied for to which the respondent agrees;
'order for financial relief' means an order under any of sections 23, 24, 24A, 24B or 27 above; and
'prescribed' means prescribed by rules of court.

Amendments—Matrimonial and Family Proceedings Act 1984, s 7; Welfare Reform and Pensions Act 1999, s 19, Sch 3.

Maintenance agreements

34   Validity of maintenance agreements

(1) If a maintenance agreement includes a provision purporting to restrict any right to apply to a court for an order containing financial arrangements, then—

(a)   that provision shall be void; but
(b)   any other financial arrangements contained in the agreement shall not thereby be rendered void or unenforceable and shall, unless they are void or unenforceable for any other reason (and subject to sections 35 and 36 below), be binding on the parties to the agreement.

(2) In this section and in section 35 below—

'maintenance agreement' means any agreement in writing made, whether before or after the commencement of this Act, between the parties to a marriage, being—
(a)   an agreement containing financial arrangements, whether made during the continuance or after the dissolution or annulment of the marriage; or
(b)   a separation agreement which contains no financial arrange- ments in a case where no other agreement in writing between the same parties contains such arrangements;
'financial arrangements' means provisions governing the rights and liabilities towards one another when living separately of the parties to a marriage (including a marriage which has been dissolved or annulled) in respect of the making or securing of payments or the disposition or use of any property, including such rights and liabilities with respect to the maintenance or education of any child, whether or not a child of the family.

35   Alteration of agreements by court during lives of parties

(1) Where a maintenance agreement is for the time being subsisting and each of the parties to the agreement is for the time being either domiciled or resident in England and Wales, then, subject to subsection (3) below, either party may apply to the court or to a magistrates' court for an order under this section.

(2) If the court to which the application is made is satisfied either—

(a) that by reason of a change in the circumstances in the light of which any financial arrangements contained in the agreement were made or, as the case may be, financial arrangements were omitted from it (including a change foreseen by the parties when making the agreement), the agreement should be altered so as to make different, or, as the case may be, so as to contain, financial arrangements, or

(b) that the agreement does not contain proper financial arrangements with respect to any child of the family,

then subject to subsections (3), (4) and (5) below, that court may by order make such alterations in the agreement—

(i)   by varying or revoking any financial arrangements contained in it, or

(ii) by inserting in it financial arrangements for the benefit of one of the parties to the agreement or of a child of the family,

as may appear to that court to be just having regard to all the circumstances, including, if relevant, the matters mentioned in section 25(4) above; and the agreement shall have effect thereafter as if any alteration made by the other had been made by agreement between the parties and for valuable consideration.

(3) A magistrates' court shall not entertain an application under subsection (1) above unless both the parties to the agreement are resident in England and Wales and at least one of the parties is resident within the commission area (within the meaning of the Justices of the Peace Act 1997) for which the court is appointed, and shall not have power to make any order on such an application except—

(a) in a case where the agreement includes no provision for periodical payments by either of the parties, an order inserting provision for the making by one of the parties of periodical payments for the maintenance of the other party or for the maintenance of any child of the family;

(b) in a case where the agreement includes provision for the making by one of the parties of periodical payments, an order increasing or reducing the rate of, or terminating, any of those payments.

(4) Where a court decides to alter, by order under this section, an agreement by inserting provision for the making or securing by one of the parties to the agreement of periodical payments for the maintenance of the other party or by increasing the rate of the periodical payments which the agreement provides shall be made by one of the parties for the maintenance

of the other, the term for which the payments or, as the case may be, the additional payments attributable to the increase are to be made under the agreement as altered by the order shall be such term as the court may specify, subject to the following limits, that is to say—

(a) where the payments will not be secured, the term shall be so defined as not to extend beyond the death of either of the parties to the agreement or the remarriage of the party to whom the payments are to be made;

(b) where the payments will be secured, the term shall be so defined as not to extend beyond the death or remarriage of that party.

(5) Where a court decides to alter, by order under this section, an agreement by inserting provision for the making or securing by one of the parties to the agreement of periodical payments for the maintenance of a child of the family or by increasing the rate of the periodical payments which the agreement provides shall be made or secured by one of the parties for the maintenance of such a child, then, in deciding the term for which under the agreement as altered by the order the payments, or as the case may be, the additional payments attributable to the increase are to be made or secured for the benefit of the child, the court shall apply the provisions of section 29(2) and (3) above as to age limits as if the order in question were a periodical payments or secured periodical payments order in favour of the child.

(6) For the avoidance of doubt it is hereby declared that nothing in this section or in section 34 above affects any power of a court before which any proceedings between the parties to a maintenance agreement are brought under any other enactment (including a provision of this Act) to make an order containing financial arrangements or any right of either party to apply for such an order in such proceedings.

Amendments—Matrimonial and Family Proceedings Act 1984, s 46(1), Sch 1, para 13; Justices of the Peace Act 1997, s 73(2), Sch 5, para 14.

36   Alteration of agreements by court after death of one party

(1) Where a maintenance agreement within the meaning of section 34 above provides for the continuation of payments under the agreement after the death of one of the parties and that party dies domiciled in England and Wales, the surviving party or the personal representatives of the deceased party may, subject to subsections (2) and (3) below, apply to the High Court or a county court for an order under section 35 above.

(2) An application under this section shall not, except with the permission of the High Court or a county court, be made after the end of the period of six months from the date on which representation in regard to the estate of the deceased is first taken out.

(3) A county court shall not entertain an application under this section, or an application for permission to make an application under this section, unless it would have jurisdiction by virtue of section 22 of the Inheritance (Provision for Family and Dependants) Act 1975 (which confers jurisdiction on county courts in proceedings under that Act if the value of the property mentioned in that section does not exceed £5,000 or such larger sum as may be fixed by order of the Lord Chancellor) to hear and determine proceedings for an order under section 2 of that Act in relation to the deceased's estate.

(4) If a maintenance agreement is altered by a court on an application made in pursuance of subsection (1) above, the like consequences shall ensue as if the alteration had been made immediately before the death by agreement between the parties and for valuable consideration.

(5) The provisions of this section shall not render the personal representatives of the deceased liable for having distributed any part of the estate of the deceased after the expiration of the period of six months referred to in subsection (2) above on the ground that they ought to have taken into account the possibility that a court might permit an application by virtue of this section to be made by the surviving party after that period; but this subsection shall not prejudice any power to recover any part of the estate so distributed arising by virtue of the making of an order in pursuance of this section.

(6) Section 31 (9) above shall apply for the purposes of subsection (2) above as it applies for the purposes of subsection (6) of section 31.

(7) Subsection (3) of section 22 of the Inheritance (Provision for Family and Dependants) Act 1975 (which enables rules of court to provide for the transfer from a county court to the High Court or from the High Court to a county court of proceedings for an order under section 2 of that Act) and paragraphs (a) and (b) of subsection (4) of that section (provisions relating to proceedings commenced in county court before coming into force of order of the Lord Chancellor under that section) shall apply in relation to proceedings consisting of any such application as is referred to in subsection (3) above as they apply in relation to proceedings for an order under section 2 of that Act.

Amendments—Inheritance (Provision for Family and Dependants) Act 1975, s 26(1).

Miscellaneous and supplemental

37   Avoidance of transactions intended to prevent or reduce financial relief

(1) For the purposes of this section 'financial relief' means relief under any of the provisions of sections 22, 23, 24, 24B, 27, 31 (except subsection (6)) and 35 above, and any reference in this section to defeating a person's claim for financial relief is a reference to preventing financial relief from being granted to that person, or to that person for the benefit of a child of the family, or reducing the amount of any financial relief which might be so granted, or frustrating or impeding the enforcement of any order which might be or has been made at his instance under any of those provisions.

(2) Where proceedings for financial relief are brought by one person against another, the court may, on the application of the first-mentioned person—

   (a)   if it is satisfied that the other party to the proceedings is, with the intention of defeating the claim for financial relief, about to make any disposition or to transfer out of the jurisdiction or otherwise deal with any property, make such order as it thinks fit for restraining the other party from so doing or otherwise for protecting the claim;

   (b)   if it is satisfied that the other party has, with that intention, made a reviewable disposition and that if the disposition were set aside financial relief or different financial relief would be granted to the applicant, make an order setting aside the disposition;

   (c)   if it is satisfied, in a case where an order has been obtained under any of the provisions mentioned in subsection (1) above by the applicant against the other party, that the other party has, with that intention, made a reviewable disposition, make an order setting aside the disposition;

and an application for the purposes of paragraph (b) above shall be made in the proceedings for the financial relief in question.

(3) Where the court makes an order under subsection (2)(b) or (c) above setting aside a disposition it shall give such consequential directions as it thinks fit for giving effect to the order (including directions requiring the making of any payments or the disposal of any property).

(4) Any disposition made by the other party to the proceedings for financial relief in question (whether before or after the commencement of those proceedings) is a reviewable disposition for the purposes of subsection (2)(b) and (c) above unless it was made for valuable consideration (other than marriage) to a person who, at the time of the disposition, acted in relation to it in good faith and without notice of any intention on the part of the other party to defeat the applicant's claim for financial relief.

(5) Where an application is made under this section with respect to a disposition which took place less than three years before the date of the application or with respect to a disposition or other dealing with property which is about to take place and the court is satisfied—

(a)   in a case falling within subsection (2)(a) or (b) above, that the disposition or other dealing would (apart from this section) have the consequence, or

(b)   in a case falling within subsection (2)(c) above, that the disposition has had the consequence,

of defeating the applicant's claim for financial relief, it shall be presumed, unless the contrary is shown, that the person who disposed of or is about to dispose of or deal with the property did so or, as the case may be, is about to do so, with the intention of defeating the applicant's claim for financial relief.

(6) In this section 'disposition' does not include any provision contained in a will or codicil but, with that exception, includes any conveyance, assurance or gift of property of any description, whether made by an instrument or otherwise.

(7) This section does not apply to a disposition made before 1 January 1968.

Amendments—Welfare Reform and Pensions Act 1999, s 19, Sch 3.

38   Orders for repayment in certain cases of sums paid after cessation of order by reason of remarriage

(1) Where—

(a)   a periodical payments or secured periodical payments order in favour of a party to a marriage (hereafter in this section referred to as 'a payments order') has ceased to have effect by reason of the remarriage of that party, and

(b)   the person liable to make payments under the order or his or her personal representatives made payments in accordance with it in respect of a period after the date of the remarriage in the mistaken belief that the order was still subsisting,

the person so liable or his or her personal representatives shall not be entitled to bring proceedings in respect of a cause of action arising out of the circumstances mentioned in paragraphs (a) and (b) above against the person entitled to payments under the order or her or his personal representatives, but may instead make an application against that person or her or his personal representatives under this section.

(2) On an application under this section the court may order the respondent to pay to the applicant a sum equal to the amount of the payments made in respect of the period mentioned in subsection (1)(b) above or, if it appears to the court that it would be unjust to make that order, it may either order the respondent to pay to the applicant such lesser sum as it thinks fit or dismiss the application.

(3) An application under this section may be made in proceedings in the High Court or a county court for leave to enforce, or the enforcement of, payment of arrears under the order in question, but when not made in such proceedings shall be made to a county court; and accordingly references in this section to the court are references to the High Court or a county court, as the circumstances require.

(4) The jurisdiction conferred on a county court by this section shall be exercisable notwithstanding that by reason of the amount claimed in the application the jurisdiction would not but for this subsection be exercisable by a county court.

(5) An order under this section for the payment of any sum may provide for the payment of that sum by instalments of such amount as may be specified in the order.

(6) The clerk of a magistrates' court to whom any payments under a payments order are required to be made, and the collecting officer under an attachment of earnings order made to secure payments under a payments order, shall not be liable—

(a)   in the case of the clerk, for any act done by him in pursuance of the payments order after the date on which that order ceased to have effect by reason of the remarriage of the person entitled to payments under it, and

(b) in the case of the collecting officer, for any act done by him after that date in accordance with any enactment or rule of court specifying how payments made to him in compliance with the attachment of earnings order are to be dealt with,

if, but only if, the act was one which he would have been under a duty to do had the payments order not so ceased to have effect and the act was done before notice in writing of the fact that the person so entitled had remarried was given to him by or on behalf of that person, the person liable to make payments under the payments order or the personal representatives of either of those persons.

(7) In this section 'collecting officer', in relation to an attachment of earnings order, means the officer of the High Court, the district judge of a county court or the clerk of a magistrates' court to whom a person makes payments in compliance with the order.

39   Settlement etc made in compliance with a property adjustment order may be avoided on bankruptcy of settlor

The fact that a settlement or transfer of property had to be made in order to comply with a property adjustment order shall not prevent that settlement or transfer from being a transaction in respect of which an order may be made under section 339 or 340 of the Insolvency Act 1986 (transfers at an undervalue and preferences).

Amendments—Insolvency Act 1985, s 235(1), Sch 8, para 23; Insolvency Act 1986, s 439(2), Sch 14.

---

40   Payments etc under order made in favour of person suffering from mental disorder

Where the court makes an order under this Part of this Act requiring payments (including a lump sum payment) to be made, or property to be transferred, to a party to a marriage and the court is satisfied that the person in whose favour the order is made is incapable, by reason of mental disorder within the meaning of the Mental Health Act 1959, of managing and administering his or her property and affairs then, subject to any order, direction or authority made or given in relation to that person under Part VIII of that Act, the court may order the payments to be made, or as the case may be, the property to be transferred, to such persons having charge of that person as the court may direct.

40A   Appeals relating to pension sharing orders which have taken effect

(1) Subsections (2) and (3) below apply where an appeal against a pension sharing order is begun on or after the day on which the order takes effect.

(2) If the pension sharing order relates to a person's rights under a pension arrangement, the appeal court may not set aside or vary the order if the person responsible for the pension arrangement has acted to his detriment in reliance on the taking effect of the order.

(3) If the pension sharing order relates to a person's shareable state scheme rights, the appeal court may not set aside or vary the order if the Secretary of State has acted to his detriment in reliance on the taking effect of the order.

(4) In determining for the purposes of subsection (2) or (3) above whether a person has acted to his detriment in reliance on the taking effect of the order, the appeal court may disregard any detriment which in its opinion is insignificant.

(5) Where subsection (2) or (3) above applies, the appeal court may make such further orders (including one or more pension sharing orders) as it thinks fit for the purpose of putting the parties in the position it considers appropriate.

(6) Section 24C above only applies to a pension sharing order under this section if the decision of the appeal court can itself be the subject of an appeal.

(7) In subsection (2) above, the reference to the person responsible for the pension arrangement is to be read in accordance with section 25D(4) above.

Amendments—Welfare Reform and Pensions Act 1999, s 19, Sch 3.

. . .

PART IV

MISCELLANEOUS AND SUPPLEMENTAL

52   Interpretation

(1) In this Act—

'child', in relation to one or both of the parties to a marriage, includes an illegitimate child of that party or, as the case may be, of both parties;

'child of the family', in relation to the parties to a marriage, means—

(a)   a child of both of those parties; and

(b)   any other child, not being a child who is placed with those parties as foster parents by a local authority or voluntary organisation, who has been treated by both of those parties as a child of their family;

'the court' (except where the context otherwise requires) means the High Court or, where a county court has jurisdiction by virtue of Part V of the Matrimonial and Family Proceedings Act 1984, a county court;

'education' includes training;

'maintenance assessment' has the same meaning as it has in the Child Support Act 1991 by virtue of section 54 of that Act as read with any regulations in force under that section.

(2)   In this Act—

(a)   references to financial provision orders, periodical payments and secured periodical payments orders and orders for the payment of a lump sum, and references to property adjustment orders, shall be construed in accordance with section 21 above;

(aa) references to pension sharing orders shall be construed in accordance with section 21A above; and

(b)   references to orders for maintenance pending suit and to interim orders for maintenance shall be construed respectively in accordance with section 22 and section 27(5) above.

(3)   For the avoidance of doubt it is hereby declared that references in this Act to remarriage include references to a marriage which is by law void or voidable.

(4)   Except where the contrary intention is indicated, references in this Act to any enactment include references to that enactment as amended, extended or applied by or under any subsequent enactment, including this Act.

Amendments—Children Act 1975, s 108(1)(b), Sch 4; Matrimonial and Family Proceedings Act 1984, s 46(1), Sch 1, para 16; CA 1989, s 108(4), (7), Sch 12, para 33, Sch 15; SI 1993/623; Welfare Reform and Pensions Act 1999, s 19, Sch 3.

INDEX

References are to paragraph numbers or the Appendix.